DRINK DAT
NEW ORLEANS

DRINK DAT

NEW ORLEANS

A Guide to the Best Cocktail Bars,
Neighborhood Pubs, & All Night Dives

ELIZABETH PEARCE

FOREWORD BY MICHAEL MURPHY

THE COUNTRYMAN PRESS
A DIVISION OF W. W. NORTON & COMPANY
INDEPENDENT PUBLISHERS SINCE 1923

Printed in the United States of America

For information about permission to reproduce selections from this book,
write to Permissions, The Countryman Press,
500 Fifth Avenue, New York, NY 10110

For information about special discounts for bulk purchases, please contact
W. W. Norton Special Sales at specialsales@wwnorton.com or 800-233-4830

The Countryman Press
www.countrymanpress.com

A division of W. W. Norton & Company
500 Fifth Avenue, New York, NY 10110
www.wwnorton.com

978-1-58157-424-1 (pbk.)

1 2 3 4 5 6 7 8 9 0

For my mother, Carolyn Pearce, who got me started
For my husband, Lee Domingue, who kept me going
For the bartenders of New Orleans, who never stop

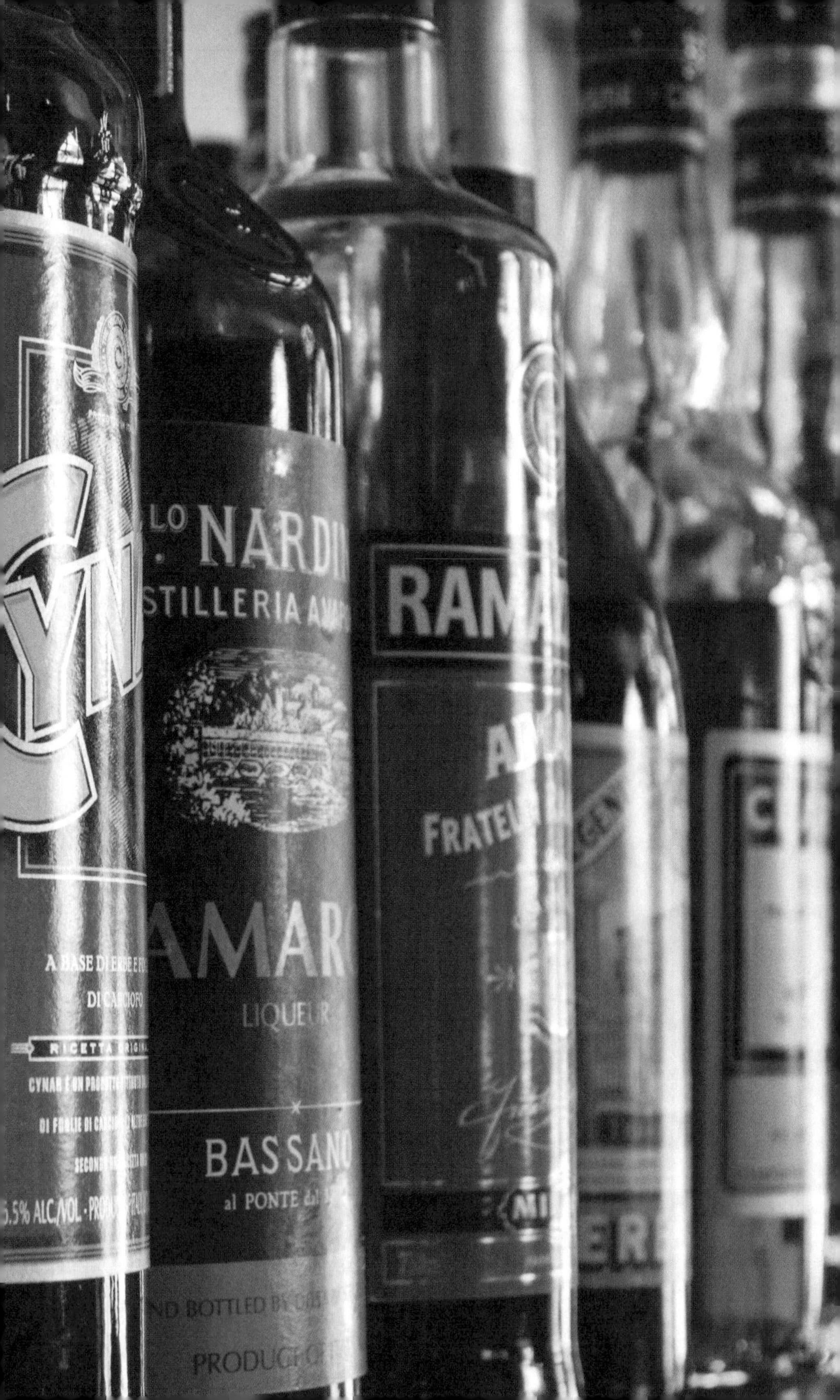
NARDI
STILLERIA
AMAR
LIQUEUR
BASSANO
RAMA
DI CARCIOFO

CONTENTS

FOREWORD

New Orleans attracts almost ten million visitors a year. When not wandering the Convention Center or being bored to death in breakout meetings, most come here to eat our food, hear our music, or drink our unique inebriations like Hurricanes, Sazeracs, Pimm's Cups, and Huge Ass Beers. *Drink Dat* will tell you all you need to know about our cocktail history and current drinking spots. No matter what level of drinking you plan to do while you're here, from sipping swanky cocktails Uptown to getting tanked on Bourbon Street, let this book be your guide.

Drink Dat is the fourth in the series of *Dat* books about all the seductive enticements that draw us those ten million visitors each year—and the first not to be written by yours truly. The very first in the series was *Eat Dat*. The offer to write that book came to me almost like the mythological hero's "call." Only rather than a burning bush or a haunting voice in the darkness of night, mine came in the form of an email in the middle of the afternoon.

Once upon a time, I had been the publisher for one of the top five publishers in America—that is, until one of the top three publishers in America bought us out. The utter disruption of my career did allow me to move from New York to New Orleans, a city I first visited in 1983 and by day two, I knew I'd found my home. Since moving to New Orleans, I've written a smattering of magazine articles, co-chaired a writers' conference, written a script for shuttle bus drivers to entertain their customers en route to the airport, sold tour tickets from inside a kiosk, worked the concierge desk at large hotels, created a miniature golf course, and got my tour guide license. I now give tours of the French Quarter and the Garden District, as well as ghost tours of this city's world-famous cemeteries.

So when a former publishing colleague emailed to ask if I wanted to write a book about the New Orleans culinary scene, I jumped at the chance. My book, *Eat Dat*, was the #1 book for Amazon . . . well, for about an hour when it first came out. *The Huffington Post* tagged it as "the #1 essential book to read before coming to New Orleans." Its success led me to do other books about all things that draw New Orleans so many visitors. *Eat Dat* was followed by *Fear Dat*—our voodoo, vampires, graveyards, and ghosts—and *Hear Dat*—our music.

My editor wanted me to do a book on our history of cocktails and current bar scene called *Drink Dat*. I backed away because I'm not much of a drinker (I like my alcohol to taste as much like Hawaiian Punch as possible). But more so because I'd come to know Elizabeth Pearce and considered her the authority when it comes to drinking in New Orleans. Elizabeth is a drinks historian and owner of Drink & Learn, where she offers tours and classes telling the history of America through booze. She's appeared on the Travel Channel and has co-written the lively and anecdotal book, *The French Quarter Drinking Companion*. She's also the Drinks Curator for the Southern Food and Beverage Museum. And, with her fiery red hair and a forever playfully puckish look that has you thinking she's about to put one over on you, Elizabeth is right out of central casting as the perfect cocktail expert. There's no way I could do better than her.

So with that, I cede the floor to my illustrious colleague. I trust she won't steer you wrong. Cheers, Salu, Nostrovia, and Bottoms up from the front of a book I know you'll find funny, refreshing, and informative.

Michael Murphy
New Orleans, 2017

INTRODUCTION

New Orleans is known for beautiful, historic architecture, amazing restaurants, and top-notch music. It is also a place where you can let your hair down, loosen your tie, and discard—albeit temporarily—your morals and judgment. A place where you can (to quote our own slogan) "Let the good times roll!" This "rolling" is almost always accompanied by alcohol.

There is certainly some truth in the portrayal of New Orleans as a city that emphasizes pleasure, though for residents, our good times are less about drinking to excess on Bourbon Street and more about drinking with friends and family. But still, our city's designation as party central has remained a prime reason that millions of visitors make the journey down here every year. And for that alone, it is worth exploring why and how that reputation came to be. So before digging into a book about the bars of New Orleans, it's worth taking a moment to understand drinking in New Orleans—what it used to be like and what it's like now.

Drinking in Yesterday's New Orleans

The city's drinking habits were impacted by three key influences: who settled here, the religions those people observed, and what life was like in the colony. A holy trinity of sources of drinking habits, if you will.

The city was founded in 1718, about the same time as the thirteen colonies were getting settled. Back in the eighteenth century, everyone drank alcohol; water made you sick, and booze didn't. But while the New England colonies were settled by Protestants, New Orleans was settled by French Catholics, and these disparate groups had very different drinking habits. Protestants believe the fate of one's immortal soul is entirely dependent on one's actions, while Catholics are resigned to an endless cycle of sin, contrition, absolution, penance, and then (surprise!) more sin. Rinse and repeat. Therefore, Puritans frowned on drunkenness while New Orleanian

Catholics accepted and even embraced it. Jean-Jacques Blaise d'Abbadie, Governor of Louisiana in 1764, once complained to King Louis XIV that "the entire colony is stupefied on tafia," which was a kind of low-grade rum.

Another reason for New Orleanians' intemperate behavior stemmed from the kind of colonist who came here. Unlike New England, which was settled by many families seeking a new life, New Orleans was largely settled by convicts, smugglers, deserters, and prostitutes who were transported to the colony instead of being sent to prison. No one was happy to be here, and many had already developed habits of ill repute, stoked by crime and alcohol. To wit, when Louis Belcourt, Chevalier de Kerlerec, became governor of Louisiana in 1753, he was told to clean up the colony of its disreputable elements. He wrote to the king, saying, "If I sent back all the bad characters, what would be left of this colony's inhabitants?"

Finally, life was pretty miserable in southern Louisiana in the eighteenth century. There was no air conditioning, the mosquitos were legion, and food supplies from France were erratic. In contrast, liquor was reliable, easily obtainable from the Caribbean and, unlike most other foodstuffs, didn't spoil. Thus, the stage was set for a city set in harsh conditions, receiving little support from the motherland, and settled by folks who were just trying to get through the day. Booze helped tremendously.

But New Orleanians' drinking habits were not determined solely by these forces. For many New Orleanians, what they drank was connected with who they were. This very French attitude extended to the food they ate as well, and whenever possible, the colonists tried to eat and drink as they had back in France. New Orleanians' reluctance to bow to an outsider's dictate about what we could eat or drink is seen very clearly in 1768. The colony was taken over by Spain, and the King of Spain told New Orleanians that they could no longer purchase French goods, but instead had to purchase Spanish goods. These "goods" included wine and brandy. One night a group of drunken locals gathered in Jackson Square to protest this proclamation, shouting, "Give us back our Bordeaux; take away the poison of Catalonia." The leaders were rounded up and hanged, and New Orleanians quickly shifted their tactics from protest to smuggling. But the message was clear: We want to drink what we like and how we like.

This sensibility, with a focus on living the kind of good life that we want to live, defined the character of the town and drew like-minded people to come here. After Louisiana became part of the United States in 1803, Americans, or "Kaintucks" as they were called, floated down the Mississippi River on barges, lured by promises of riches in the bustling port city and fueled by jugs of whiskey they sipped en route. Once they arrived, they cut loose in the bars and bordellos that lined the river alongside the wharves. By the mid-nineteenth century, the city was seen as a place to party, a place where people danced at balls all night and drank at taverns well into the next day.

After the Civil War, the city's businessmen tried to clean up the town in order to attract new industry. In a moment of surprising pragmatism, they acknowledged they could not actually eradicate vice, so they opted instead to contain it. Thus was born Storyville, named for Alderman Sidney Story, its creator. In 1897, a thirty-eight–block section of downtown New Orleans (including parts of the French Quarter and Tremé neighborhoods) was cordoned off and zoned for legalized gambling and prostitution, activities inexorably connected with saloons and drinking. To no one's surprise, the fortunes of Storyville soared, and its existence merely cemented New Orleans as a place where every manner of vice was gathered in one handy locale for your pleasure. Of course it wasn't all vice. Out of this den of iniquity came jazz, which blossomed in the district as pianists and bands provided the soundtrack for everyone's sins.

Storyville was shut down in 1917 at the request of the United States government, which worried that servicemen sent through the port on their way to serve in World War I were leaving the city with not only memories of good times but also venereal diseases. Its closure indirectly led to the creation of Bourbon Street as we know it today. Up to that point, Bourbon Street was merely another commercial street in the French Quarter, but when Storyville shuttered, many of the area's clubs relocated to Bourbon Street, and, by the end of World War II, it became a thriving entertainment district.

By the twentieth century, New Orleans had become a traveler's destination. Two key municipal decisions anchored New Orleans's reputation as a place to cut loose: The first was a lack of closing times for bars, and the second was the legalization of open containers. Most cities require the party to end, but in New Orleans the lights can stay on all night. Furthermore, you don't even have to be inside to do your drinking, which means the good times could literally roll up and down the street all night.

But the truth is, while these laws certainly enhance a visitor's pleasure, ultimately they were not created for tourists. They were implemented in response to the citizens and the kind of life we want to create here. For example, most visitors think that open containers are only permitted on Bourbon Street, or in the French Quarter, but that is not the case. Unlike other cities that have created "entertainment districts" that permit open containers for a segmented portion of the city, New Orleanians can take their go-cups with them throughout the entire city. One of the pleasures of living in New Orleans is being able to come home after work, take your dog for a walk, and visit with your neighbors, all while sipping on the beer/wine/cocktail of your choice. The go-cup is ubiquitous across the city; it is one of our defining artifacts.

Drinking in Today's New Orleans

For me and many New Orleanians, it took Hurricane Katrina to make us fully appreciate the drinking freedoms New Orleans afforded us and how those liberties were an integral part of our experience in our city. We missed having a bottle of wine with our picnic at a park. We forgot about Sunday blue laws and showed up empty-handed to dinner parties. We puzzled at friends who downed three shots of whiskey in the ten minutes before last call, and we chafed at bartenders who would turn on all the lights just when the conversation was getting good. We wondered if we would ever again be able to take our drink outside of a bar and savor the last few sips on our walk home. These may all seem petty, trivial moments, but their sum represents a way of drinking here that informs how we live the rest of our lives. And when we returned to New Orleans, we all talked about how much we missed them. And we did so, of course, over a drink, in a bar.

Katrina brought many changes to the city, and some fear that New Orleans has lost some of what made it so distinctive. But when it comes to how we drink and the role that drinking plays in our lives, not much has changed. Like our ancestors back in 1768, we continue to be defined by what and how and where we drink. What we consume makes us who we are, whom we consume it with shapes our relationships, and the places where we do it remain places of conviviality that only close when the last patron goes home.

How to Use This Book

You'd think the endless parade of nights spent drinking and taking notes would have been the hardest part of writing this book. And while my liver may be a little worse for wear, that honor actually belongs to the difficult process of deciding which venues should and shouldn't be included in this volume. After all, New Orleans has hundreds of establishments that could be termed a "bar," and I have so many wonderful memories from tippling in the vast majority of them.

I started trimming the herd by eliminating music venues. While almost all of these places feature a bar, their focus is not on cultivating a drinking environment. (If music and venues interest you, check out Michael Murphy's book in this series, *Hear Dat*.) Similarly, I have omitted strip clubs since, let's face it, you're paying for something other than the drinks. At $9 a Bud Light, you damn well should be.

Restaurants proved to be their own bugbear. As dining habits have changed, the distinction between what makes a bar and what makes a restaurant have blurred. Restaurants have been upping their drinking game, so there were many contenders. Additionally, new liquor permits in New Orleans are difficult to obtain, and many require one to open a restaurant instead of just opening a bar. Maintaining this restaurant/bar permit means that food sales must exceed drink sales. Several "restaurants" in the French Quarter tried to work around this requirement—I once ordered a whiskey and soda, and the guy behind the bar told me to just ignore my receipt, which said "chicken wings." Predictably, many of them have been busted and then shuttered. A restaurant only made the cut if their bar offers something notable, such as a large list of a particular spirit, or if their cocktail program is particularly respected.

Deciding among neighborhood bars was also trying. I endeavored to include bars in each neighborhood that manage to embody something essential about New Orleans, no matter how ephemeral that quality may be.

Truthfully, I had already visited almost every bar in this book when I got my contract, but I revisited them all again in order to really see each place, in order to be fair. I'm sure there will be folks who take issue with the inclusion or exclusion of some bars. That's the nature of list-making. But I think it's a good list. Or, certainly, a good list to begin with.

Taking on a project like this requires moral support, as well as someone willing to do the drinking when I needed to stay sober-ish to take notes. You will see mention of my fiancé, Lee, throughout this book. We were engaged at the start of this book and, thankfully, that's still the case. I could have written this book without him, but I'm glad I didn't have to.

Famous Drinks of New Orleans

Before we take a tour of the best bars this fine city has to offer, it's worth noting some of the famous cocktails that put New Orleans on the map in the first place. You may not find these concoctions on the menu at every establishment, but give them a try if you see them and taste a bit of the city's history. They are arranged, more or less, in the order of their creation.

THE SAZERAC

In 2008, the Sazerac was declared the official cocktail of New Orleans. This spicy, liquorice-flavored mixture of sugar, rye whiskey, Peychaud's bitters, Herbsaint, and a lemon twist has its home at the Sazerac Bar in the Roosevelt Hotel. But its origins lie in a pharmacy just a few blocks away in the French Quarter, near the intersection of Royal and St. Louis streets.

There, in 1832, Antoine Amédée Peychaud prepared and sold his family's bitters recipe. In the nineteenth century, many pharmacists mixed their own bitters, which were used to treat all manner of ailments. To make his version more palatable, Peychaud mixed his anise-flavored bitters with brandy and sugar. Peychaud's medicinal drink became widely popular and soon crossed over from something you would order from a pharmacist to something you would order in a bar.

One such location was the Sazerac Bar, so named because it served *Sazerac du Forts et Fils Cognac*. Patrons would order the mixture made with the namesake cognac, and soon the drink became known as a Sazerac. In the 1880s, a terrible disease destroyed France's vineyards, creating a cognac shortage, so the owner of the Sazerac Bar swapped out the cognac with more easily obtainable American rye whiskey. He also added a little absinthe to the cocktail. When absinthe was banned in the United States in the early 1900s, a local absinthe maker, Marion Legendre, created a substitute called Herbsaint, and the current recipe of rye, sugar, Peychaud's and Herbsaint was set.

During Prohibition, the Sazerac Bar closed and Marion Legendre stopped producing his Herbsaint. Peychaud's Bitters, however, remained available as a "medicine." When that dark time ended, the bar relocated to the Roosevelt Hotel, and Legendre restarted his Herbsaint business. By the mid-twentieth century, the Sazerac had become a bit of a relic, something people might make on special occasions or during holidays. But as the craft cocktail gained momentum in the early twenty-first century, the Sazerac saw a resurgence, and it now appears on menus across the city.

Not only has the drink remained popular, but so have the ingredients. Russ Bergeron, beverage director at the Sazerac Bar, once commented that if you open the liquor cabinet in most New Orleans homes, you will find bottles of Peychaud's Bitters and Herbsaint. "They may be a little dusty," he says, "but they will be there!" You should drink at least one Sazerac cocktail while you are in New Orleans, and the Sazerac Bar is as good a place as any to start.

THE PIMM'S CUP

The Pimm's Cup shows up in so many New Orleans bars that many visitors think the drink is a New Orleans creation. This would come as a surprise to James Pimm of London, who invented the drink's signature ingredient in the 1830s. So, how did a British beverage become a mainstay of New Orleans drink menus? In the late 1940s, Joe Impastato took over running the Napoleon House, the restaurant that had been in his family since the 1920s. During his tenure, according to family lore, what was primarily a sandwich shop slowly became a bar, which led to an increase liquor sales. Joe didn't like to see people get too drunk or rowdy in his establishment, so he encouraged them to sip on less alcoholic beverages such as the Pimm's Cup.

The cocktail is made with lemonade, cucumber, and the British liqueur Pimm's #1, a gin-based spirit containing a secret mixture of herbs and liqueurs. Served in a collins glass and garnished with a cucumber, the Pimm's Cup is a perfect thirst quencher for New Orleans summer drinking. It satisfies without getting you hammered. Pimm's Cup sales at the Napoleon House continue to soar, and the bar is now the Pimm's company's largest North American account.

RAMOS GIN FIZZ

The Ramos Gin Fizz is a foamy concoction of gin, lime, lemon, orange flower water, cream, soda, and an egg white. The egg white is key to creating the drink's proper frothy consistency, as are the fifteen minutes the bartender spends shaking the drink to create that foam. The drink is a New Orleans original, created in the 1880s by Henry C. Ramos at his Imperial Cabinet Saloon at the corner of Carondelet and Gravier Streets, in what is now the Central Business District. There, the Ramos Gin Fizz gained fame; in 1888, Ramos sold five thousand gin fizzes in one week. In 1907, Ramos moved his establishment down the street a few blocks to a new joint, The Stag.

In the book *Famous New Orleans Drinks and How to Mix 'Em*, Stanley Clisby Arthur writes that at The Stag, "the corps of busy shaker boys behind the bar was one of the sights of the town during Carnival, and in the 1915 Mardi Gras, 35 shaker boys nearly shook their arms off, but were still unable to keep up with the demand."

With the passage of the Volstead Act—which created Prohibition—Ramos, a law-abiding man, closed up shop. Interestingly, he started another kind of mixing business: He ran a paint store. He died in 1928, before the repeal of Prohibition and, sadly, before he could mix another drink. Fortunately for posterity, he did allow his closely guarded recipe for the Ramos Gin Fizz to be published and, after Prohibition, the drink found a new home at the Sazerac Bar, where it remains a favorite.

CAFÉ BRÛLOT

The origins of Café Brûlot are murky at best. Antoine's Restaurant claims that its first owner, Antoine Alciatore, invented the drink in the 1890s. Rivals of Antoine's put forth stories involving creators as disparate as the pirate Jean Lafitte and the "Voodoo Queen," Marie Laveau. While it does seem that Antoine's popularized the New Orleans version of this flamed coffee drink, its origins actually lie in France.

There, bon vivants would soak a sugar cube in brandy, set it aflame, and drop the caramelized lump into their coffee—in French, "brûlot" translates as "burnt brandy." Today in New Orleans, the drink is only made at a few old-line Creole restaurants, where it is made tableside. The waiter places cloves, cinnamon sticks, and citrus peel in a specially crafted brûlot bowl that can withstand high heat. Brandy and sometimes Grand Marnier are added, and then the mixture is set aflame. The moment of ignition is spectacular, and often the waiter will use a special ladle to lift the brandy out of the bowl and drizzle it onto the tablecloth, creating a ring of fire around the bowl. Eventually, the fire is extinguished with the strong coffee.

If you want to try this drink, you will need to go to Galatoire's, Arnaud's, Antoine's, or Commander's Palace. There may be a few more places that serve it, but not many. If you don't want to commit to an entire meal at these locations, some places will let you order just the drink, particularly if you visit during slow times.

Also, keep in mind that you can't order individual servings of Café Brûlot; it only comes by the bowl. So, if you are dining alone, feel free to offer cups of the coffee to your fellow diners. You'll be sure to win friends. John Ringling of Ringling Brothers Circus famously said of Café Brûlot, "What better than to taste the pleasures of heaven while beholding the flames of Hell?"

LA LOUISIANE

The La Louisiane, a mixture of rye, sweet vermouth, Bénédictine, and Peychaud's Bitters, was once the signature cocktail of the now defunct restaurant and hotel of the same name. Historians dispute the date of its invention, but all acknowledge it was the restaurant's answer to the more popular Sazerac.

The restaurant, which opened in 1891, was owned and run by Fernand Jules Alciatore (of Antoine's Restaurant fame) until the early twentieth century. It was Alciatore who began to keep a guest registry that he dubbed "The Golden Book," which, over time, burst with signatures from prominent guests, including presidents, titans of industry, and even Harry Houdini. The list speaks to the popularity of New Orleans as a destination before and during Prohibition. When legendary mobster "Diamond Jim" Moran purchased the restaurant, he decorated the space even more extravagantly, covering the ceilings with Baccarat chandeliers. He was even known to surprise prominent patrons with a diamond-studded meatball.

Once its namesake restaurant closed, the La Louisiane's popularity declined and—like the Roffignac—it lost its home base. But the La Louisiane has recently had a resurgence, and I've seen the drink on menus across town, notably at the 21st Amendment bar, which is located in the former La Louisiane restaurant's building.

ROFFIGNAC

In the late 1790s, Count Louis Philippe Joseph de Roffignac arrived in New Orleans and soon became a very busy guy. He was a state legislator, a director of the State Bank of Louisiana, and a soldier in the Battle of New Orleans. Roffignac later served as mayor from 1820 through 1828, creating the city's first fire department and bringing cobblestones and gas lighting to the streets of the French Quarter.

Unfortunately, Count Roffignac died before his namesake drink was invented. According to *The Mascot*, the local paper of Storyville, the drink started popping around the 1890s. It later gained fame as the house cocktail at Maylie's, one of New Orleans's top restaurants in the early twentieth century, rivaled only by Antoine's among the city's elite. When Maylie's doors shuttered in 1986, the Roffignac lost a regular home, and its popularity soon faded.

The most well-known recipe for the Roffignac comes from Stanley Clisby Arthur's recipe in *Famous New Orleans Drinks and How to Mix 'Em* (1937). Arthur calls for whiskey, sugar, soda, and raspberry syrup, though the syrup can be substituted with red hembarig. That last ingredient is likely an English mispronunciation of *himbeeressig*, a German raspberry vinegar syrup. To modern palates, vinegar seems most appropriate for salads, but it was a fairly common ingredient in cocktails in the nineteenth century, especially if perishable citrus fruits like lemons or limes were hard to come by. Though the drink is hard to find nowadays, Paul Gustings at the Empire Bar at Broussard's Restaurant often has some homemade hembarig syrup handy. It's worth seeking out this unusual drink created for Mayor Roffignac.

GRASSHOPPER

The Grasshopper was invented by Philibert Guichet, the owner of Tujague's Restaurant and Bar. In the early twentieth century, Mr. Guichet entered a cocktail contest in New York and took home second place for this mixture of crème de menthe, crème de cacao, and cream. Tujague's serves the drink today with a twist on the original recipe: Bartenders add a brandy float on top to cut through all of that sweetness. It's a drink that has remained popular among New Orleanians, many of whom have dined at Tujague's with family through the years and even drank Grasshoppers as children. (Yes, there's alcohol in it, but if you skip the brandy float, there's not much.) The drink's sweetness means most people prefer to drink it at the end of a meal, in lieu of dessert. However, its low alcohol content also makes it perfect for daytime sipping, when you want to imbibe but still stay on your feet.

VIEUX CARRÉ

The original name for the French Quarter was *Vieux Carré*, French for "Old Square." Locals still use this name for the city's oldest neighborhood, but the pronunciation drops almost all pretense to the French language, and the result is closer to "voo kah-ray."

Regardless of how you say it, you should definitely order the drink that bears its name. The drink was invented in the 1930s by Walter Bergeron, the head bartender at the Monteleone Hotel. "It was created as a tribute to the different ethnic groups of the city: the Benedictine and cognac to the French influence, the Sazerac rye as a tribute to the American influence, the sweet vermouth to the Italian, and the bitters as a tribute to the Caribbean." The result is similar in taste to a Manhattan, but smoothed out by the cognac and Bénédictine.

Most sources, including the Monteleone Hotel website, claim the drink was invented in 1938, which is puzzling since it appears in the 1937 edition of Stanley Clisby Arthur's book *Famous New Orleans Drinks and How to Mix 'Em*, a popular cocktail resource found on most New Orleanians' bookshelves. Mr. Arthur observes: "This is the cocktail that Walter Bergeron, head bartender of the Hotel Monteleone cocktail lounge, takes special pride in mixing. He originated it, he says, to do honor to the famed Vieux Carré, that part of New Orleans where the antique shops and iron lace balconies give sightseers a glimpse into the romance of another day." Vieux Carrés are best sipped while sitting at the slowly circling Carousel Bar, placing a reorder every third rotation.

THE HURRICANE

The Hurricane was invented in 1942 at Pat O'Brien's bar. It features heavy pours of dark and light rum, mixed with fruit juice. Its creation owed less to inspiration than to necessity, because Pat O'Brien had a bar full of rum that no one wanted to drink.

Back during Prohibition, Americans were happy to drink anything they could get their hands on, including bathtub gin, moonshine, and rum. But given their choice, they preferred whiskey. When Prohibition ended, whiskey sales soared, and those of other spirits plummeted. It was then that Pat O'Brien opened his namesake bar, Pat O'Brien's, just off Bourbon Street in 1933. All of his patrons were thirsty for the whiskey they had been denied during the Great Mistake.

Not long after he opened his bar, Great Britain entered World War II. This moment was a difficult time for bar owners. Because of Prohibition, there was very little American whiskey available to drink. Most of it lay aging in barrels. Instead, American whiskey lovers drank whiskey from Canada and Great Britain. With Great Britain fighting the war, the Scotch and Irish whiskey supply dried up, and Pat O'Brien could only offer Canadian and American whiskeys. When the United States joined the war, all American whiskey distillers had to stop making whiskey and start making airplane fuel, as well as other products that required industrial-grade alcohol. American whiskey supplies plummeted. The only easily obtainable spirit was rum from the Caribbean.

Pat O'Brien's liquor distributors required the bar to purchase twelve cases of rum for every case of whiskey it bought. Faced with an abundance of booze no one really wanted to drink, Pat O'Brien held a contest among his bartenders to invent a new cocktail using up all of this rum. Thus was born the Hurricane, named in honor of Pat O'Brien's tenure as a Prohibition speakeasy owner, during which his bar's password was "storm's brewing." The original hurricane recipe is delicious, featuring dark and light rum, as well as passion fruit and lime juice. As the drink grew in popularity, the bar cut corners, and now it's made from a mix, resulting in a sugary concoction closer to Kool-Aid than a cocktail. It's worth seeking out local rum–focused bars like Latitude 29, Tiki Tolteca, Cane & Table and The Black Duck, all of which make the original recipe and use real juice.

HAND GRENADE

The Hand Grenade is touted as the strongest drink on Bourbon Street, and it is named for the *effect* it has on your body, mind, and (presumably) soul. Though the recipe is a closely guarded secret, its melon flavor indicates a presence of Midori, which helpfully masks the taste of its other ingredient: overproof booze. It was invented by Pam Fortner and Earl

Bernhardt, who served it at their bar at the New Orleans World's Fair in 1984. After the fair closed, the pair opened several bars on and near Bourbon Street, the most famous of which is Tropical Isle. The Hand Grenade was one of the first drinks on Bourbon Street to be served in its own specialty plastic cup, which encouraged folks to carry it throughout the French Quarter. If you are leery of such a strong concoction, you can instead sample Hand Grenade–flavored peanuts or condoms, both of which are available at the various Tropical Isle outlets.

The Tropical Isle website strongly suggests you don't drink more than three. Personal experience compels me to tell you it's really best to stick to one.

CHAPTER 1

The French Quarter and Algiers

The French Quarter is the epicenter of New Orleans. The food, the art, the music, the sensibility of the city—they all began here. When locals who live in other neighborhoods come here, they may grumble about the tourists, the lack of parking, and even the smell of Bourbon Street, but the truth is, we all love the French Quarter. We have all made some amazing memories here, and we have all spent at least one night here that we simultaneously look upon with regret and/or pride.

The French founded New Orleans in 1718, and in 1721 they laid out the grid for its oldest neighborhood, then called the Vieux Carré, meaning "Old Square." France controlled the colony until 1763, when they turned it over to Spain. In 1788, a large fire swept through the city, burning over 80 percent of the buildings. Spain rebuilt the town, and most of that architecture remains, so the area called the French Quarter is actually full of Spanish architecture. Every visitor has heard of this neighborhood, and it's where most spend their time, but people often confine themselves to about eight or ten blocks near Canal Street and the Mississippi River. That's a shame, because the French Quarter is much more diverse than its famous Bourbon Street would indicate. It's a neighborhood that has lured bohemians and artists, and it remains a haven for creative people.

Just across the river from the French Quarter, and accessible by a ten-minute ferry ride, lies Algiers, the second-oldest neighborhood in the city. Originally a staging ground for immigrants and later enslaved workers brought from Africa, this neighborhood grew in charm and wealth in the mid-nineteenth century. Algiers Point, the area at the ferry's landing, is a time capsule of that era, with rows of perfectly preserved, ornately embellished homes. The view of downtown New Orleans from the ferry and Algiers Point is not to be missed, but if you do go, make sure to bring exact change for the ride ($2 each way) and check the timetable so you won't miss the last boat back.

The French Quarter

Bourbon Street: All of it

This is not a typical entry for this guide, but Bourbon Street is not a typical place. You may think that in condensing the many bars of Bourbon Street into one entry, I am giving them short shrift, essentially telling you to avoid this strip. I am not. It's an essential part of the full New Orleans experience. But while some bars on this street do differentiate themselves from the rest—and they are presented later in this chapter—on the whole, going out on Bourbon Street does not consist of separate experiences in discrete establishments. Instead, your night (and/or morning) is truly the sum of its parts, and many of those parts don't occur inside a bar. At some point the entire street is, in fact, your bar.

First, a little history. Bourbon Street has not always been a tourist destination, nor a haven of bars and clubs. For most of its existence, it was a residential area that gradually developed into a commercial zone. If you were from out of town in the nineteenth century and looking for a good time, you didn't visit Bourbon Street. Instead, you either stayed near the wharf, drinking with sailors, or headed to Storyville, a section of the French Quarter and Tremé where prostitution and gambling were legally sanctioned from 1895 to 1917. When the city closed Storyville, several of the club owners relocated their establishments to Bourbon. But it wasn't until World War II brought thousands of thirsty servicemen looking for one last hurrah in a city known for a good time that Bourbon Street's character as a party street began to develop.

In the 1970s, with the advent of cheap plastic cups, bars began selling drinks through windows to patrons on the sidewalk, which increased pedestrian traffic. This was also when the city closed the street to cars in the evenings, cementing its place as a never-ending street party. As you stroll, remember that Bourbon Street grew organically and remains its own living self. There is no Bourbon Street committee that has planned this place.

So that's what the street was. Let's talk about what is. Three-for-one drinks. Neon. Historic buildings. Strip clubs. Music clubs. Souvenir shops. Restaurants. Bars. Street performers. Homeless people. Parents with children. Drunks. Bartenders. Hawkers. Cops. Cover bands. Jazz bands. Karaoke. Second lines. Urine. Vomit. Litter. And liquor. Everywhere.

As you walk, you'll encounter the same types of bars up and down Bourbon Street over and over. The first are music venues, which host cover bands playing classic-rock favorites. These spots offer drink specials all day and night, usually three for one. Bear in mind, these places can sometimes stiff you as they fill your enormous go-cup with more soda than whiskey. If you stick with beer, you can be assured you are getting what you paid for. Many of these venues also have balconies where patrons can hang out and gawk at passing pedestrians below. You might be tempted to cajole someone into baring flesh for beads, though if it's not Mardi Gras, you may be disappointed with the results. None of these spots are really better than the others. Let the cover band be your guide. If they are playing a song you like, go in. You may end up staying all night.

Then come the places where you aren't meant to linger. Bourbon Street is best experienced while strolling with a drink in hand, and many places that line it are set up to facilitate just that. Frozen daiquiri shops and walk-up bars offer drinks that keep pedestrians well fueled for the night. Frozen daiquiris are like slushies with alcohol. They come in more flavors than you can imagine in colors not present in the natural world. If it's slow, the bartenders there will often let you have a sample, since the flavors "WTF" or "Panty Dropper" might be hard to describe. Other walk-up bars offer drinks served in absurdly shaped or absurdly large cups: big-ass beers, fishbowls, jesters, hand grenades, and, of course, hurricanes are all on offer.

Finally, Bourbon Street is also home to numerous strip clubs, but I'm not including them in my definition of bars, because you're not going there to drink. You're mostly going for the view.

Locals have lots to say about the street, and most of it is negative: It's touristy. It's vulgar. It doesn't embody what New Orleans is really about. It's inauthentic. It's crowded. It smells. Unsurprisingly, locals often avoid

Bourbon Street. Instead, they smugly say "Oh, I only go to Frenchmen St./St. Claude. That's where the real New Orleans is." But this rejection means they miss out on a very special adventure that happens in their own backyard, an amazing intersection of private fun and public experience. I have to admit, I once held their attitude, but then one night, while out with friends, we decided to hit Bourbon Street just for fun. And you know what? We had a really good time. We drank and danced and walked along the strip with all the other folks who have traveled to do this very same thing. Bourbon Street is teeming with people who are all there to enjoy themselves, cut loose, maybe have a little too much to drink, stay out later than the bars back home would ever allow, dance, laugh, and wake up feeling terrible but not so awful that they don't want to do it again. Bourbon Street is not a place to start your night. You probably shouldn't go there totally sober. And you certainly don't have to stay there. But you should definitely go, and, as the Buddhists say, go with an open heart.

21ST AMENDMENT

725 Iberville St. • (504) 378-7330
www.21stamendmentlalouisiane.com
HOURS 3 p.m.–midnight Mon–Thu; 2 p.m.–1 a.m. Fri and Sat; 3 p.m.–11 p.m. Sun
HAPPY HOUR from opening til 6 p.m.

Decorated with images of Prohibition protesters and mobsters, 21st Amendment sits across from the madness of the line at the Acme Oyster House. Its name honors the repeal of Prohibition, and its vibe echoes that celebratory time in the city. The bar is located in the former La Louisiane Restaurant and Hotel, home of the La Louisiane cocktail. The bar makes a good one, and it also turns out quality standard classics like a Bee's Knees and a twist on a French 75. The 21st Amendment is a cocktail bar in the midst of a crowd that may not know much about them. Their menu gives detailed descriptions of the flavor profiles of each signature drink, with key elements italicized for eyes that might be already a bit blurred from nearby Bourbon Street.

The bar hosts a variety of live music each night, so while the drink prices may seem a bit steep, once you factor in what is essentially cover for the band, it's a good value. If you are standing in the eternal line at Acme, you may as well be drinking something delicious while you wait. Have your friend hold your spot and return with a La Louisiane.

THE ABBEY BAR

1123 Decatur St. • (504) 523-7177

No website

HOURS Open 7 days a week, 24 hours a day

NO HAPPY HOUR

Cash only

The Abbey (or, for locals, "The Scabby") is a grimy cathedral to late night (and early morning) drinking. Stained glass windows on the wall and above the bar are there for decoration only. There is no natural light in the Abbey, save for the sliver peeking through the door. It's best that way. People come here to get very drunk with friends or friends they have yet to meet. They come for the $3.50 generous glass of well whiskey and $2 pints of High Life. The Abbey welcomes all, from the solo drinker who wants to nurse a cold one with minimal social interaction to the bachelor party that got lost while traveling from the strip clubs to Frenchmen Street.

The origin of The Abbey is a surprising one. The Abbey began its life as a bohemian cafe run by Jo Ann Clevenger, now the James Beard award–winning proprietor of the Upperline restaurant. She wanted to create an artists' haven, and she brought in the stained glass windows and other decor. She also used to fly in the Sunday *New York Times* to encourage intellectuals to patronize her cafe. At the time, The Abbey was the only place in town where you could get the Sunday *New York Times* on Sunday. People used to venture all the way from Uptown to read the paper at the Abbey. My, how times have changed.

The jukebox has something for everyone. Fleetwood Mac and Meat Loaf join Gwar and the Cramps, and many CD compilations sport handwritten labels. Don't be surprised when patrons sing/shout/yell along.

According to the bartender, the Abbey serves as a final resting place for several patrons whose ashes now reside behind the bar, per the deceased's

The stately bar at Arnaud's French 75

request. This unkempt, beloved chapel seems a fitting spot for a barfly to spend eternity, nestled among the bottles, basking in the holy glow of the stained glass and beer signs.

ARNAUD'S FRENCH 75 BAR

813 Bienville St. • (504) 523-5433
www.arnaudsrestaurant.com/french-75/
HOURS 5:30 p.m.–11 p.m. Sun–Thu; 5:30 p.m.–midnight Fri and Sat
NO HAPPY HOUR ("We're just happy")

French 75 is where I would have the last drink of my life. Well, one of them. French 75 is where I would have the last fancy drink of my life. The beer and shot would be around the corner at the Erin Rose. French 75 is not a historic location; it opened in 2003. The bar, however, dates to the mid-nineteenth century, installed here by Arnaud's when they converted a "gentleman's waiting room" into this charming, tiny saloon.

French 75 is best enjoyed if you have had a hectic day and need tending to. Settle into one of the leopard-print loveseats stationed between the cheeky monkey lamps, and enjoy the table service. Bartender Chris Hannah is the star of this spot, but all of the staff here are top notch. I have never had an even mediocre cocktail here, and I drink here as regularly as my pocketbook allows. The cocktail menu is always full of surprises, but don't be afraid to order a favorite standard; this is the place to get that perfect, classic daiquiri or Manhattan. While you wait for your drink, make sure to read your cocktail napkin's drinking quotes, including my favorite from Mark Twain: "Sometimes too much to drink is barely enough." If you are lucky to get Chris as your bartender and it's a slow night, you can learn more than you ever imagined about classic drinks, including, of course, the French 75. Some other bartenders make it with gin, but Chris prefers to use brandy and even has on offer a small, well-researched treatise confirming brandy as its definitive spirit. The drinks here are not cheap, but when you think of the price as rent on a chair, it's one of the town's most economical ways to rejuvenate and face the raucousness of the French Quarter.

BAR TONIQUE
820 N. Rampart St. • (504) 324 6045
www.bartonique.com
HOURS noon–3 a.m. 7 days a week
HAPPY HOUR noon–5 p.m.

Ten years ago, North Rampart was where you headed if you wanted to score some cheap drugs or a hooker. Or both. But North Rampart, like much of New Orleans, has been changing. And Bar Tonique was one of the trailblazing establishments that helped turn a seedy strip into a thoroughfare with a little more traffic and a little less, ahem, "traffic," one cocktail at a time. If you open a craft cocktail joint in what some still called "the hood," you better make it either worth the trek for cocktail fans or affordable to folks used to getting a Crown and Coke. And coke. Tonique did both.

Bar Tonique runs drink specials every day of the week, from Pimm's Cups to Caipirinhas. If you're more of a wine buff and less into the booze, you're in luck: Wine selections are impressive. Though the bartenders are more laid back here than at some of the more formal (stuffy) establishments

Bar Tonique

in town, they all shake an equally mean drink. When it's 2 a.m. and I'm not yet ready to switch to beer, I know I can come here for a well-made standard. I wish that the area behind the bar wasn't tiny. Even when they are slammed, only two bartenders can fit behind that magic square of booze. This means that when the bar fills up on the weekends, the wait for a drink can get ridiculous. Better to visit during the afternoons or do as many service industry folks do and hit it in the later part of the evening, when you can take a seat at the bar with bartenders from across town. It's a great place to start or finish your night.

BEACHBUM'S LATITUDE 29

321 N. Peters St. • (504) 609-3811

www.latitude29nola.com

HOURS 3 p.m.–11 p.m. Sun–Thu; noon–11 p.m. Fri and Sat

HAPPY HOUR 3 p.m.–6 p.m. Sat–Thu; noon–6 p.m. Fri

The concept of tiki sprang from the cocktail shakers of two men: Ernest Raymond Beaumont Gantt, aka "Don the Beachcomber," and Victor

The tiki-focused bar at Beachbum Berry's Latitude 29 with its sculptural rum map

"Trader Vic" Bergeron. It reached its apogee in the 1960s when tiki restaurants proliferated around the country, and patrons could dine under bamboo-thatched roofs, watch exotic Polynesian-themed dances, and sip on rum cocktails made from secret recipes. The movement lost steam in the 1970s, and by the 1980s, many tiki restaurants had closed. The man to thank for tiki's renaissance is Jeff "Beachbum" Berry. Berry is not one to "toot his own conch shell," as he says, but Jeff literally wrote the book on tiki by tracking down and saving many original tiki recipes that would have otherwise been lost to time. Back in the 1980s, when no one cared about tiki except Berry and a few other diehard fans, he hunted down former bartenders and spent hours wheedling these old-timers to share private notebooks with proprietary recipes. Sometimes, it took years for Berry to find the original recipe for a drink. After publishing several definitive volumes, Berry's next step was to put it all into practice and open a bar. New Orleans was the perfect place to do so, not only because of our strong drinking culture, but because Don the Beachcomber was from here.

Latitude 29 (the latitude of New Orleans) is a tiki lover's delight. Tucked in the narrow space of the Hotel Bienville, the bar is packed with tiki decor that is too well crafted to be just kitsch. Hand-carved tiki statues created especially for the restaurant welcome drinkers. Behind the bar is a "Map of Tiki," with statues dotting the myriad islands that contributed to the movement's creation. Go ahead and start your journey. If you've never had a well-made tiki drink, you may be surprised at its complexity. This is not the jungle juice you drank at that unfortunate spring break party. Try the traditional Mai Tai or Nui Nui or a house creation like its namesake, the Latitude 29, or the Pontchartrain Pearl Diver. Skip the cloying disappointment of a Pat O'Brien's hurricane and try one at Latitude (one half of the Hurricane Two-Step, completed at Tiki Tolteca down the block). If you are a rum fan, you will love drinking your way down their highly curated rum list, which is organized by flavor profile. Latitude's kitchen offers modern twists on the "Polynesian" fare of the 1950s, and the homemade taro chips are a perfect accompaniment to the drinks. Jeff explains, "A classic pre-Prohibition cocktail usually maxes out at three ingredients. It's like a song, while a classic tiki drink is more like a symphony, a polyphonic composition balancing up to fourteen different ingredients. I think that complexity is what's attracting today's mixologists to the genre—it's a way to stretch themselves, to flex their muscles." Make sure to spend some time at Latitude 29 and enjoy its symphonic delights.

BLACK PENNY

700 N. Rampart St. • (504) 304-4779
www.facebook.com/Black-Penny-363706927153453
HOURS 4 p.m.–4 a.m. Mon–Wed; 2 p.m.–4 a.m. Thu–Sun
NO HAPPY HOUR

Black Penny used to be a bar called The Ninth Circle. It was a dive. Your mother would not be happy if you drank there regularly (or worked there). The first time I went to the newly opened Black Penny, I was astounded. It was, well, clean. I could see the floor, the walls. I asked the bartender how long it took for them to scrub away the sin, and he replied, "Sin doesn't come off, just dirt." Black Penny is part of a renaissance on Rampart, where sketchy bars are turning into neighborhood bars. Where people can go after work, or late at night, and not lose their wallets or their souls.

Black Penny is a welcoming spot, set on the corner of Rampart and St. Peter, and when its door is opened up to Rampart Street foot traffic, it's a beacon of hospitality. I can only imagine that once the streetcar is rolling down Rampart in late 2016, the view from the bar will be even better.

Black Penny's specialty is canned beers, or, I should say, delicious canned beers. As the craft movement has grown in the United States, so has the quality and availability of canned craft brews. Operating a bar in the French Quarter requires nothing less than an acknowledgement that every drink should be a walking drink, and the Black Penny has embraced that fact. Lee, beer aficionado that he is, usually takes his beer in a glass, but he is also a big fan of the go-cup and admires Black Penny's commitment to offering a wide, portable beer selection. Though there is no regular kitchen, the Old Portage pop-up on Saturdays offers a rotating selection of hearty food that pairs well with beer.

But Black Penny isn't just a beer bar. You can get a great cocktail here, especially a whiskey one, and especially if Jonathan is working. I'm thinking in particular about a "Manhattan tasting" I had one night, featuring three different whiskeys, when I encouraged my fellow patrons to taste them all and cast their votes. I think Rittenhouse whiskey won. Actually, hell, everyone won that night. Black Penny is the kind of bar where conviviality and a lack of boundaries are at least tolerated, if not encouraged. It's a friendly place to pop in for a go-cup or to stay in for many rounds. Round after round, it's lots of whiskey and beer in a can. America!

THE BOMBAY CLUB
830 Conti St. • (504) 577-2237
www.bombayclubneworleans.com
HOURS 4 p.m.–11 p.m. 7 days a week
HAPPY HOUR 4 p.m.–7 p.m. 7 days a week

If there aren't enough British men's clubs in your life—replete with wood, leather, and portraits of the aristocracy—you can fill that void at the Bombay Club. Prince Albert gazes down, patiently and benevolently, upon the crowd sitting in leather sofas and enjoying the sounds of traditional jazz.

Bartender Blake Kaiser pours a martini at the Bombay Club

The square bar anchors the room, radiating a solid, masculine presence. Its cocktail menu covers three centuries, but shines the spotlight on vintage drinks like the Aviation and Sidecar and a variety of martinis. The nightly music (no cover) features some really classy jazz acts to match the classy air. Some guests enjoy dinner in booths discreetly tucked behind velvet curtains, while others take their drinks to the small patio off the side of the bar. The darkness and low ceilings of the Bombay Club make it feel cool when the summer sun is beating down and cozy and warm when winter makes its brief appearance. It is a haven, a respite, from the hordes of Bourbon Street. Prince Albert would approve.

BOURBON HOUSE

144 Bourbon St.
(504) 522-0111
www.bourbonhouse.com
HOURS 11 a.m.–10 p.m. 7 days a week
HAPPY HOUR 4 p.m.–6 p.m. 7 days a week

Bourbon House, located near the corner of Bourbon and Iberville, offers a welcome change from the neon located just outside its doors. Golden lanterns soar above the bar, which seats twenty-two bourbon-loving patrons. Guests can sample over one hundred brands of American whiskeys, including bourbon, rye, and Tennessee whiskey. I recommend trying one of their flights, a nice way to move across their list and still stay on your feet. But Bourbon House also makes solid, classic whiskey cocktails, as well as their own versions of city favorites like the Streetcar—a riff on the Sidecar—made with bourbon and crème de cassis. Is it hot outside? Do you want something to cool you off? Instead of imbibing one of the lurid, frozen concoctions just down the block, try the house specialty, the Frozen Bourbon Milk Punch. It's a bit sweet for me, but an extra shot of bourbon adds balance and bite.

It's worth taking two minutes to join the New Orleans Bourbon Society (NOBS). Your free membership gets you a free pour of the bourbon of the month, which you can sample on the spot. The card invites you to sample all of the bourbons proffered. I'm not sure what the trophy is for completing the task, but I kind of want to find out.

A bartender puts the finishing touches on an Old Fashioned at Dickie Brennan's Bourbon House

BOURBON O

730 Bourbon St. • (504) 571-4685

www.bourbono.com

HOURS noon–midnight Sun–Thu; noon–1 a.m. Fri and Sat

NO HAPPY HOUR ("They're all happy")

Most bars in the French Quarter seem to cater to either Mardi Gras bead-wearing revelers looking for the strongest neon drink money can buy, or more upscale cocktail connoisseurs looking for the most creative drinks money can buy. Bourbon O caters to both. Bourbon O is one of the only bars on Bourbon Street that I know of where you can order a Vieux Carré and a Jaeger Bomb at the same time and know that both will be equally satisfying. In fact, they have an entire menu of drink "bombs" from which to choose, some of which are riffs on classic cocktails like the "Death in the Afternoon Bomb" and the "Last Word Bomb." Bar manager Cheryl Charming (and she certainly is!) said that when she took over the bar, she insisted that she be able to serve the needs of the many different customers who come through her doors.

Knowing about the bar's two doors is actually the key to understanding her patrons. One door opens to the lobby of the Bourbon Orleans Hotel, a building dating to the nineteenth century and serving an upscale clientele. The other door opens to Bourbon Street, serving, well, everyone else. The decor of the bar also seems to find a happy middle ground. Its sleek, black marble bar and candlelit lounge area are elegant escapes from Bourbon Street, and the shiny Bourbon O Bar sign above the stage evokes a 1950s glamour, back when tourists came to Bourbon Street to see burlesque performers like Evangeline the Oyster Girl and Blaze Starr. It feels both classy and a bit showy. The bar's menu is a delight, designed like a newspaper that is "republished" with every changing season. Though their cocktails may seem a bit pricey ($12–$15), they are all well crafted. Cocktail fans will want to be sure to order a Ramos Gin Fizz, just so they can see the "shaking machine" Charming has installed to ensure the drink is well mixed. The nightly jazz band (no cover) keeps the room lively. I love the intersection of highbrow and lowbrow in this bar, and when I return, I'm totally doing that "Last Word Bomb."

Brennan's beautiful new bar with view of their courtyard

BRENNAN'S

417 Royal St. • (504) 571-4685

HOURS 9 a.m.–10 p.m. Mon–Fri, 8 a.m.–10 p.m. Sat–Sun

HAPPY HOUR 2–7 p.m. Tue–Fri

5 p.m. every Friday champagne sabering in the courtyard

Brennan's is a venerable New Orleans restaurant. Since 1946, visitors to the city have made a pilgrimage to its famed doors to partake in traditional brunch dishes like Eggs Sardou and Eggs Hussarde. Unfortunately, over the last few years, the quality of the meals there declined, and the restaurant's reputation deteriorated. Visitors still made the trek, but many left disappointed. In 2015, a different member of the Brennan's family tree, Ralph Brennan, acquired the property and gave it a multimillion-dollar renovation. Not only did he spruce up the space and (more importantly) improve the food, he also created a bar whose elegance matches the restaurant's storied past.

Brennan's original bar, located at the entrance to the restaurant, was more of a stand-up bar, with no room for stools or comfortable drinking. The new bar is a lovely space further into the restaurant, with a view of the building's courtyard. Visitors can luxuriate in cushy seats at the bar, surrounded by a gorgeous, kaleidoscopic-colored bird mural. Or, when the weather is nice, they can take their drinks into the lush and well-appointed courtyard.

Ralph grew up working in the restaurant and told me how happy he is to be back here, not only running it but doing so with his children. His affection for the place is evident in the effort put into the renovation.

Tuesdays through Fridays they have champagne happy hours, and Friday afternoons, you can see them saber the champagne to remove the corks. What to drink? This is a historic, old-line Creole restaurant. Order a favorite classic. NB: The Old Fashioned is the muddled-fruit kind, not the "mixologist kind" with only one perfect Luxardo cherry. My mother would approve.

CAFE LAFITTE IN EXILE

901 Bourbon St. • (504) 522-8397

www.lafittes.com

HOURS 24 hours a day 7 days a week

HAPPY HOUR 4 p.m.–9 p.m.

This bar's original location was a few blocks down Bourbon Street toward Esplanade Avenue at what is now Lafitte's Blacksmith Shop. In the mid-1940s, saloon keeper Tom Caplinger turned what was an abandoned blacksmith shop into a bar he called Cafe Lafitte's. It was a spot that attracted bohemians and artists, including Noel Coward and Truman Capote. It was also very welcoming to gay patrons. Caplinger encouraged artists to hang their work on the walls, turning the bar into a gallery. In 1953, when it was discovered there was no clear title to the bar, the building was sold at auction and Caplinger was booted out. He moved his establishment down the street and opened Cafe Lafitte's in Exile. He carried with him his hospitable attitude, and today Cafe Lafitte's claims the title as the oldest continuously operating gay bar in the United States.

Guests can enjoy hanging out on its generous balcony and peering down on confused tourists who are probably looking for the other Lafitte's and wondering if maybe they've wandered too far. The balcony also offers a view of campy movies, projected nightly on the Clover Grill's wall across the street. Lafitte's Bourbon Street address also means it's a little touristy, though the tourists in question are mostly gay patrons who have made the pilgrimage to this historic spot. This isn't to say there aren't locals, but the atmosphere reflects the vibrant nature of its Bourbon Street location. This isn't a neighborhood bar.

Regardless of your gender and orientation, Lafitte's certainly worth popping into, if only for its historic significance. You can think about how far our country has come in embracing all kinds of people, as well as how far we have to go, musings that always go down better with a drink.

CANE & TABLE

1113 Decatur St. • (504) 581-1112

www.caneandtablenola.com/

Cane and Table's bar with its rustic, Caribbean aesthetic

HOURS 3 p.m.–midnight Mon–Thu; noon–midnight Fri;
10:30 a.m.–midnight Sat and Sun
HAPPY HOUR 3–6 p.m. 7 days a week

I'm pretty sure I've seen a bar like Cane & Table in a James Bond movie. I kept expecting 007 to stroll in and order a daiquiri (in lieu of his usual martini) before joining a villain or beautiful woman (or both) at one of the tables along the patina-rich walls. The Caribbean vibe manifests throughout the bar, from the French doors leading to the lush patio to the fresh pineapples placed on tabletops and along the marble bar. The glow from mismatched, cloudy chandeliers casts a warm light. Drinking at Cane & Table feels like you are drinking in another country, and that's saying something in New Orleans, a city that already feels about as far from the United States as you can go without a passport. This sense of journeying away from the mainland is echoed by a compass rose placed in the middle of a menu that does its utmost to steer guests in the direction that best fits their drinking needs.

The bartender insisted that everyone, not just "cocktail nerds," can have a good time at Cane & Table. When a bar is located on the busy end of Decatur, it needs to be able to satisfy the many kinds of patrons who may walk through the door. But he also admitted that while he can make a vodka and soda for those who want one, Cane & Table is as much a rum collector and aficionado bar as anything else. Cane & Table treats rum with a reverence usually reserved for whiskey in this country. All of the bartenders here are incredibly knowledgeable about the spirit, well-schooled by rum connoisseur and co-owner Nick Dietrich. They can rhapsodize about their drinks and rums in a slightly geeky way. Some may find that level of knowledge off-putting, but I think it's rather endearing. For centuries, rum has been scorned as the drink of pirates and spring breakers getting hammered on the beach. It's nice to see it spoken of with such adoration and passion. Cane & Table is a not a tiki bar but a rum bar, a distinction that matters if you are looking for a Zombie or Mai Tai. If that is your bag, you should head up Decatur to either Latitude 29 or Tiki Tolteca. Instead, Cane & Table's focus is on what they call "proto-tiki," rum drinks that inspired or led to tiki. Feel free to consult the map/menu, but I also recommend putting yourself in the hands of the very talented folks behind the bar, who can transport you to other lands while you stay firmly planted on your stool.

CAROUSEL BAR & LOUNGE

214 Royal St. • (504) 523-3341
www.hotelmonteleone.com/entertainment/carousel-bar/
HOURS 7 days 11 a.m.–until
NO HAPPY HOUR

There are few drinking experiences equal to having a round (!) at the Carousel Bar. Slip into one of the gilded chairs and circumnavigate the mirrored column under the carousel's canopy as your bar stool slowly spins around the room. Here, bartenders feverishly mix up Pimm's Cups and Old Fashioneds to satisfy a thirsty crowd that often spills out into the lobby. Think the bar is packed? It used to be worse. For years, the Carousel's giant bar was the hotel's only bar and filled the room just off the lobby. In 2012, the hotel removed the back wall and opened the bar to create a huge lounge

The ornate, famed Carousel Bar in the Monteleone Hotel

dotted with cozy groupings of sofas and chairs. They also added another bar in the back to take the pressure off the carousel.

What to order as you slowly wind around the room? A classic, of course. You can try the Vieux Carré, a riff on the Sazerac created at the Monteleone as a rival for that classic drink. If you are a fan of Ernest Hemingway, sample either a Death in the Afternoon or a traditional shaken Daiquiri. Both were favorites of the author, a regular guest at the hotel. Or you can just stick with a shot of whiskey, the tipple of choice of Truman Capote, who claimed to have been born here. (His mother lived here while pregnant with the author, but she did manage to get to the hospital in time to have little Truman.)

It takes about fifteen minutes for the bar to complete a circle, so you want to make your drink last for two rounds, ideally three. If you want to assure yourself a spot at the carousel, you have a better shot if you go midweek and midday. On the weekends, the bar brims with locals and visitors, and the room's ambient noise rises and dips in time with the breaks of the live jazz band that plays most evenings. I've had many a good afternoon and evening at the Carousel Bar, and as I write this, I am looking forward to one weekend in particular. I'm getting married in late July, and my guests and I are staying at the Monteleone. I imagine we will be spending more than one evening drinking at the Carousel Bar. I wonder if brides get any leeway in securing a spot at the bar. I'll have to find out.

CHART ROOM

300 Chartres St. • (504) 522-1708
No website
HOURS 11 a.m.–4 a.m.
NO HAPPY HOUR
Cash only

The Chart Room is one of my favorite day-drinking stops in the Quarter. I used to come here because the drinks were cheap and strong (they still are). Cash only establishments are notoriously affordable in that regard. But now I come because in the middle of this very touristy part of the French Quarter, this place feels like a bar from another neighborhood in New Orleans.

The bartenders and patrons are local, and they sound it. The jukebox, filled with CDs from Allen Toussaint, Irma Thomas, Fats Domino and Dr. John, further contributes to that New Orleans sound. My favorite table is at the corner of Bienville and Chartres, which opens onto the street. During the day, you can scoot your chair so that you are practically sitting on the sidewalk. It's a nice contrast to stay planted at the intersection of the cool darkness of the bar (even in daylight, it's always dark) and the bustling brightness of the tourist-filled sidewalk. If you can't stay, it's still worth stopping in for a walking-around drink.

COSIMO'S

1201 Burgundy St. • (504) 522-9715
www.facebook.com/cosimosbar
HOURS 4 p.m.–2 a.m. Mon–Thu; 2 p.m.–4 a.m. Fri–Sun
HAPPY HOUR from opening til 7 p.m.

Most visitors to the French Quarter tend to forget that it is an actual neighborhood: a place that has two schools, grocery stores, a post office, and people who live there. Visitors tend to overlook this because their experience is usually confined to the more touristy areas of the Quarter, especially that part of the Quarter bounded by Canal, St. Ann, Decatur, and Bourbon Streets. But if you are willing to step away from that well-beaten path, you can mingle with plenty of people who call America's playground their home. One of the best places to do that is at Cosimo's.

Cosimo's is located in the most residential quadrant of the Quarter. Don't come looking for a praline shop or a plastic alligator souvenir here. It is also the only bar for several blocks in any direction, a notable fact given the high density of bars in other parts of the neighborhood. Its presence at this end of Burgundy is a welcome surprise for folks who are just meandering around and stumble upon it. Cosimo's is open late and also has a pretty late kitchen, and unlike most French Quarter bars, it is full of locals. Some of them are headed to work (there's lots of service industry folks here) and some have just finished up their day. There may be some tourists, but they probably arrived here by accident or because they are sleeping at an Airbnb nearby.

Cosimo's opened in 1934, right after the repeal of Prohibition, and it's remained a beloved watering hole since then. Their weekly crawfish boils (when they are in season) always draw a crowd, and you will often find just as many people standing outside the bar visiting as you may find inside. The interior hasn't changed much since the 1930s. The mahogany bar has been worn down by thousands of arms leaning over to grab a beer. The long mirror behind it and the numerous beaded pendant lights bring soft illumination to the dimness. There's a pool table and dartboard for folks in the mood to play, but my favorite touch is the sconce lamp that hangs above the center of the bar's mirror. It reminds me of a porch light, and it's always on. I like to think of Cosimo's as the kind of place that is always there, leaving the light on for its neighbors to come in for a drink.

THE DUNGEON
738 Toulouse St. • No phone
HOURS vary, but if you go after midnight, they should be open.
www.thedungeonneworleans.com/home.html
NO HAPPY HOUR

I grew up an hour from New Orleans, and I started going out in the city with friends when I was in high school. We usually stuck with Bourbon Street, mostly because we knew where it was, and in the 1980s, it was easy to drink there underage. But there were other places in the Quarter whose names carried with them auras of the forbidden, places that would have made our parents worry if they knew we were there. One was The Crystal, a dark, goth bar that played The Cure and Morrissey. It is now the rather cheerful Spitfire Bar. The other was the Dungeon. We heard all sorts of sordid things about this place. There were live sex acts, including a whole room devoted to S&M. There were skeletons, chains, Satanic rites. It didn't even open until midnight. You can imagine where our suburban minds went. When I finally went to the Dungeon, I had to admit that while it didn't match up with my adolescent fantasies, it was, and still is, a pretty fucking cool bar.

You enter down a long, narrow side alley, leaving vulgar Bourbon Street for something a little darker. The music can really define the evening at the Dungeon. Sometimes it's more old-school (Lynyrd Skynyrd) but most nights/mornings, it lives up to its reputation as a metal bar with Judas Priest and Iron Maiden in heavy rotation. The atmosphere feels like a really well-done haunted house. The decor has not changed since I came here in college: black walls, chains, skeletons. There is an area for some S&M, though I've never seen any activity. Signs throughout the club proclaim "NO VIDEO/NO PHOTOS," so presumably there's some occasional action that no one wants recorded.

These days the Dungeon seems more like a place to chill and listen to something besides the typical Bourbon Street mix of Journey and Jimmy Buffett. If you can score seating in the cage at the end of the bar, do so. It's easy for the bartender to keep an eye on you and keep your drinks refilled, and hell, when else are you going to drink in a cage?

EL LIBRE

508 Dumaine St. • (504) 309-2699
www.ellibrenola.com
HOURS 9 a.m.–4:30 p.m. Mon; closed Tue; 9 a.m.–11 p.m. Wed–Thu; 9 a.m.–midnight Fri–Sat; 9 a.m.–11 p.m. Sun
NO HAPPY HOUR

Bartender Bazil Zerinsky pours a Daquiri at El Libre

If Cane & Table down the street is where James Bond rubbed elbows with the hoi polloi of the Caribbean underworld, then El Libre is the rum bar where he meets his local contact. Set under the banner of the Cuban flag, this joint serves up big flavored drinks that belie its tiny size. Bar manager Konrad Kantor describes it as a space that evokes Cuban nostalgia combined with a New Orleans appreciation for well-made cocktails and sandwiches. This is quite a set of shoes to fill in a town that claims the Sazerac, the muffaletta, and the po' boy.

Kantor says the size of the venue actually determined the concept, one hashed out after several rounds at Latitude 29, a place that surely had some subconscious influence on El Libre's ultimate incarnation. El Libre pours twenty-five rums and not much else, nudging people to try classic Cuban drinks like a traditional daiquiri or mojito. Kantor does keep orgeat syrup on hand to make a mean Mai Tai—not exactly Cuban, but delicious nonetheless. Guests can head upstairs to some very tiny loft seating, but I preferred to hang out at the bar, chatting with the very amiable Kantor.

His commitment to his craft is evident, and in a bar with such a limited menu, every detail matters. For instance, he makes all of his grenadine and changes the flavors seasonally. In winter, the pomegranate base is spiked with orange zest, cinnamon and cloves. In summer, the flavors change to lime and orange flower water. A lot of people claim to dislike rum, but Kantor believes that's because they had a bad experience with it. I agree with this assertion, remembering one very unfortunate night at Pat O'Brien's that put me off rum for years. Kantor and his crew are trying to win folks back to the rum camp. If the comments from the lively bachelor party who took over the upstairs one night was any indication, they are succeeding. There's not much room for decor in El Libre, but the little wall space boasts a cardboard cutout of Ernest Hemingway as well as his quote: "Live the full life of the mind, exhilarated by new ideas, intoxicated by the romance of the unusual." A good motto for life. A good motto for a bar.

EMPIRE BAR AT BROUSSARD'S

819 Conti St. • (504) 581-3866
www.broussards.com/news/
empire-bar/647
HOURS 4 p.m.–10 p.m. 7 days a week
HAPPY HOUR 4 p.m.–7 p.m. 7 days a week

The original owner of Broussard's was a big fan of Napoleon and named the Empire Bar in honor of the general. His brandy appears in a list of signature cocktails created by booze star and head bartender Paul Gustings. Drinks from Paul are often full of surprises. His Ramos Gin Fizz (made in less than five minutes with a secret technique) is one of the best in the city, as is his Sidecar

Bartender Paul Gustings serves absinthe at the Empire Bar at Broussard's

made with Armagnac. He delights in making obscure, historic drinks. His milk punch, for example, is nothing like the creamy Brandy Milk Punch that appears on so many New Orleans menus, though he will make you one of those if you specify so. Instead, his version is unusually light and refreshing. He recently created a flight of five New Orleans signature drinks, serving two ounces each of a Sazerac, a La Louisiane, a Vieux Carré, a Roffignac, and a Pousse-Café. Paul looks like a grumpy Santa Claus, but if you are interested in going down a deep rabbit hole of obscure eighteenth and nineteenth century drinking, he is your guy. The happy hour is worth trying to hit, not only for its drink specials but its tasty snacks, in particular the crab sliders. The bar is small and perfectly fine for sitting and visiting with Paul, but weather permitting you should take your drink outside. Take a seat under the 150-year-old wisteria or at one of the wrought-iron tables in the middle of the space. Broussard's was once part of a larger property built in 1837 by Samuel Hermann. The gate in the back wall of the courtyard leads to the Hermann Grima historic home, which is open for daily tours. It's easy to spend a late afternoon in the Broussard's courtyard, enjoying your drink and pretending you are a wealthy nineteenth-century merchant, like Samuel Hermann, away from the hustle of the city.

ERIN ROSE

811 Conti St. • (504) 523-8619
www.erinrosebar.com
HOURS 10 a.m.–7 a.m. 7 days a week
HAPPY HOUR 10 a.m.–2 p.m.

The Erin Rose is one of my favorite French Quarter bars, and when I tell people this, they assume I am finishing my nights there, because while it's not a twenty-four-hour bar, the Rose (as fans call it) keeps late hours. But for me, I prefer day-drinking there, before the crowds come, when the bar is a lovely mixture of tourists, locals, and neighbors, all coming to start their day with a drink.

The Rose opens every day at 10 a.m. As bartender Rhiannon Enlil has observed about that opening time: "No one has been drinking here through the night. Everyone starts from 'Good morning!'" Most begin with the Rose's "Wake Up and Live" specials. I'm partial to the Irish Coffee, either

The Erin Rose with its delightful, eclectic decor

frozen or hot depending on the weather. The prices allow you to be magnanimous, buying a round or two for anyone who came with you. But the Rose is also a good place to go have a drink alone. Enlil is a great host, casually introducing patrons to each other. Perhaps a local patron has restaurant recommendations for the tourist sitting nearby. Perhaps another local gets a recommendation for a plumber, while another has a quick nip before running errands. Enlil enjoys the variety of folks who come through the door, and slower mornings allow her to visit with each of them. It's that welcoming ease that most characterizes the Rose. Owner Angie Koehlar puts it succinctly: "She's twenty-five feet off Bourbon Street, but you'd never know it. You can walk in and feel like you can settle down and be at peace."

When I spoke with Koehlar, something stuck out from our conversation: She constantly referred to the Erin Rose as "she," as in, "She was born a long time ago," and, "She became ours fifteen years ago." Both Enlil and Koehlar, and frankly the entire staff of the Rose, think of the bar as this living, breathing entity. Not a place where you party, but someone who parties with you. Not a place to escape to, but someone who offers you comfort. And this attitude toward to the Rose seems to spring from its original owner, Jim Monaghan, who also ran Molly's at the Market. Koehlar credits Monaghan with teaching her how to listen to customers, how to pay attention to what they needed, and how to shape the bar to offer that. The Rose has lived up to that goal. Angie notes that when Jim passed on and the bar became theirs, "It was like we just had a child. She became our baby." For many years, the Koehlars had to stay up late with the Rose, just like you do with an infant, but now, "She tells us: 'Mom and Dad, I got this. Why don't you go sit down and have a drink.'" As Koehlar says with pride, "She is a grown woman; she's a beauty."

GALATOIRE'S 33

215 Bourbon St. • (504) 335-3932
www.galatoires33barandsteak.com/home
HOURS 5 p.m.–10 p.m. Mon; 11 a.m.–10 p.m. Tue–Sun
HAPPY HOUR 5 p.m.–7 p.m. Mon–Thur

When you are a 100-year-old restaurant, the presumption is that you will stick with what you know and not try anything new. How nice that Galatoire's ignored this paean in 2013 and opened Galatoire's 33, an oasis of class and comfort in the middle of gaudy, crass Bourbon Street. Unlike its sister restaurant, whose upstairs bar is usually crowded with folks waiting for a table, this bar—really almost a lounge—is happy to accommodate patrons who are looking for a drink (or three), and who may not want a bite at all. The cocktail menu reflects the steakhouse theme: classics, classics, classics. Old Fashioneds and Sazeracs perfectly suit the formal yet comfortable decor. You can also get a delicious traditional daiquiri, a nice contrast to the frozen sugar bombs pouring out of venues all up and down the street. And just because Galatoire's 33 is a place with tradition doesn't mean it is stuffy. Even if you are in a t-shirt and shorts, you can pop in here and enjoy a taste of history.

GOLDEN LANTERN
(A.K.A. TUBBY'S GOLDEN LANTERN)

1239 Royal St. • (504) 529 2860
No website
HOURS 24 hours a day 7 days a week
HAPPY HOUR 8 a.m.–8 p.m.

Elegant digs at Galatoire's 33

Early on in my New Orleans tenure, I was out late in the Quarter with my roommate. We were tipsy and hungry, so I suggested we visit a Chinese restaurant I had recently noticed called the Golden Lantern. He quickly disabused me of that notion. The only thing you are taking out of the Golden Lantern is a delicious Bloody Mary.

Though the name may speak otherwise, there's no chinoiserie in the

Golden Lantern. Instead of silk dragons and paper screens, the decor is typical French Quarter bar: exposed brick, dim lighting, and a worn, wooden bar top. Though the Golden Lantern is definitely a gay bar, it is also a neighborhood bar. It's typical to see folks who live nearby stop in for an after work cocktail, visit with the bartender, and bemoan the rising Airbnb presence in the Quarter (or similar local problems). The bar can get hopping on the weekends, especially during drag shows and Saints games, which have more in common than most believe. If you are around before a drag show, you should definitely arm yourself with plenty of dollar bills to tip the talent. The shows are unforgettable, no matter how hard you try. The Golden Lantern attracts some of the more "senior" queens, few of whom ever bother to memorize the words to the songs they're lip-synching. Instead, they choose to do what a friend calls "eat pudding," which is just moving your lips in time with the music. No one is fooled but everyone is entertained. Golden Lantern drag shows are best chased with a whiskey, neat.

GOOD FRIENDS

740 Dauphine St. • (504) 566-7191
www.goodfriendsbar.com
HOURS 24 hours a day, 7 days a week
HAPPY HOUR 4 p.m.–9 p.m.

Back in the 1990s, ladies loved going to "fern bars." These spots were allegedly classier than regular bars, as they were filled with plants (ferns) and other amenities appealing to women. Ladies could hang out there, order a chardonnay, and not be looked at askance by the bartender. Good Friends is a kind of fern bar, though in this case, the ferns are neon, perched on the four corners of the bar. While you could probably order a chardonnay, most patrons stick with vodka and soda.

Good Friends is a gay bar and occupies a corner on what is affectionately called "The Fruit Loop," a circle of gay bars in the lower end of the French Quarter. But it is also a neighborhood bar and the patrons range across gender, age, and sexual orientation depending on the time of day and season. Unlike many gay bars whose clientele tend to skew male, Good Friends has a nice mix of men and women. The bar's balcony offers a tranquil escape and shade under its jaunty umbrellas, and both it and the downstairs bar are places you can always count on as relatively quiet places to visit and catch up with friends. Good Friends is a consistently welcoming place, made even sweeter by its signature drink, the Separator, a kind of frozen White Russian/Brandy Alexander that tastes fantastic on a hot day. When they ask if you want it topped with whipped cream, the answer is always yes.

HARRY'S CORNER BAR

900 Chartres St. • (504) 524-1107
No website
HOURS 10 a.m.–2 a.m. 7 days a week (may be open later at bartender's discretion)
NO HAPPY HOUR
Cash only

Harry's is a great neighborhood bar located in the heart of what most people don't think of as a neighborhood: the French Quarter. But unlike many bars just a few blocks away that cater to out of towners, Harry's patrons are mostly local. Artists who work on Jackson Square, musicians who play on Bourbon Street, waiters and bartenders who keep crowds well fed and well watered, all eventually congregate at this mecca for locals.

An artist friend of mine, Katie, usually stops in at Harry's after she has packed up her art on Jackson Square and is headed home for the day. She also told me that during Saints games, many artists will post a sign next to their art, saying, "I'm at Harry's Bar watching the Saints. If you want to buy something, just call me." She said that invariably, at least one of her artist friends will get a call from a customer, run the two blocks to Jackson Square, make a sale and return to the bar, rarely missing even one play.

Harry's is most certainly a favorite because of its reasonable drink prices, but it is also popular because of its easy charm. Its jukebox is full of classic rock and old country, and the bartender will usually walk over and fill the room with Elvis Presley and Loretta Lynn when the music runs out. All of the bartenders are friendly that way. Unlike a lot of newer places that are staffed with kids barely old enough to drink, Harry's bartenders are all "of a certain age." They've seen a lot and they know a lot, but they aren't jaded or grumpy. They are just happy to pour you a rum and Coke and tell you everything they love about New Orleans, and if you sit there long enough, the regulars next to you will join in with suggestions of their own.

HERMES BAR

725 St. Louis St. • (504) 237-4144

www.antoines.com

HOURS 11 a.m.–11 p.m. Mon–Thu; 11 a.m.–12:30 a.m. Fri and Sat;
11 a.m.–8:30 p.m. Sun

HAPPY HOUR 4 p.m.–7 p.m. 7 days a week

The Hermes Bar is located in Antoine's, the oldest restaurant in New Orleans and the second oldest restaurant in the United States. Dining at Antoine's, a posh affair, requires the time to linger over many courses and a wallet to handle the bill. Drinking at the Hermes Bar is a perfect stand-in for those who lack the time or money to commit to a full-on dinner at Antoine's but

Drinking among the Carnival jewels at the Hermes Bar

still want to bask in its old line Creole glow. People have been drinking here since 1840, a worthwhile reason to imbibe, if you need one. If you need another, check out the decor. The bar is named for one of the more upscale Mardi Gras krewes. Hermes (pronounced "herm-eez" in New Orleans) is the longest-running, night-parading krewe in the city, and its unofficial head-quarters is Antoine's. Glass cases of krewe memorabilia line the walls, full of photographs, crowns, scepters, and lovely historic invitations harkening back to days before Evite ruled our inboxes. Though the Hermes bar certainly exudes a posh air, late afternoons and evenings here can turn lively, even rowdy. Even the rich like to get drunk. The room fills with a healthy mix of tourists and locals. When the weather is warm, you can spot locals by their seersucker and tourists by their cargo shorts. You are in a historic bar, so try for the former if you decide to pay the bar a visit. It's best to stick to classics like a Sazerac, a Side Car or, when summer approaches, to quaff a Pimm's Cup. Whatever you choose, take a minute to sit back and enjoy the history. They've got it in spades.

KINGFISH

337 Chartres St. • (504) 598-5005
www.kingfishneworleans.com
HOURS 10 a.m–10 p.m. Sun–Thu; 11 a.m.–11 p.m. Fri–Sat
HAPPY HOUR 3 p.m.–6 p.m.

Huey "The Kingfish" Long was governor of Louisiana from 1928 to 1932, later serving as the state's U.S. senator and even running for President. He was a populist with a big personality, famous for his slogan "Every man a king." He was also a big fan of drinking. During his tenure as governor during Prohibition, he was asked by the mayor of Atlanta what he was doing to uphold the Eighteenth Amendment. Long replied, "Not a damn thing."

In particular, he was a fan of drinking at the Sazerac Bar in New Orleans. So much so that he purportedly had Airline Highway built so he would have a straight shot from the state capitol in Baton Rouge to the bar. He even took the Sazerac's bartenders with him on trips in order to educate bartenders in New York about the proper way to make a Ramos Gin Fizz.

The Kingfish Bar is a tribute to its namesake's personality. His portrait dominates the bar, and the menu reflects the kind of drinks Long would have enjoyed, like a French 75 and Mint Julep, as well as classics with a twist like the Amelia Earhart, the bar's version of the Aviation. The bartenders are a treat. Even when the crowd is deep, they remain a friendly bunch, keeping the chaos well managed and turning out consistently well made drinks at a bar whose surface is covered with wine cork sections, a nod to its robust wine list. The bar is often busy, and the lively crowd would have suited Long. I can just seen him in his white suit, sipping a Ramos Gin Fizz under the ceiling fans' gentle breeze. It would be fitting for him to hold court in a bar, a place where every man (and woman) can be a king.

LAFITTE'S BLACKSMITH SHOP

941 Bourbon St. • (504) 593-9761
www.lafittesblacksmithshop.com
HOURS 10 a.m.–late
NO HAPPY HOUR

Lafitte's Blacksmith Shop contends it is the oldest operating bar in the United States. This may be true. It's definitely the oldest building in New Orleans operating as a bar; the edifice was erected around 1722. Local hero and privateer Jean Lafitte probably drank here, since his brother lived around the corner. I make no pronouncements on the legend that his ghost still haunts the fireplace; you can check that out for yourself.

Lafitte's fills up in the evenings, when lubricated visitors crowd around the piano, lustily belting out "House of the Rising Sun." I prefer to arrive at the bar earlier in the day, when there's a better chance of snagging one of my favorite tables near a window. There, you can eavesdrop on the buggy drivers who invariably pause at the bar and recount the fabled story of Jean Lafitte. Yours is not to wonder at the truth of their tales. Distinguishing between truth and fiction has never been a high priority in the French Quarter.

Twilight arrives and the bar's only illuminations are candlelight and the cigarette machine, both of which offer their own kind of romantic glow. When the piano bar gets too rowdy, the tiny, side patio offers quiet sanctuary. Lafitte's makes a passable hurricane, but touts their frozen voodoo purple drink as their "special." Maybe one of those is all you need to catch a glimpse of the ghost of Jean Lafitte.

MOLLY'S AT THE MARKET

1107 Decatur St. • (504) 525 5169
www.mollysatthemarket.net
HOURS 10 a.m.–6 a.m.
NO HAPPY HOUR

I went to college at Louisiana State University, about an hour from New Orleans. My roommate and I would often make the trek to New Orleans to do a little weekend drinking, and Molly's was one of our regular stops. It was easy to find, perched across from the statue of Joan of Arc in all her gilded glory. And it seemed, to us, a quintessential New Orleans bar. Unlike the joints we frequented in Baton Rouge, it was notably democratic. Folks of all ages, shapes and colors could be found drinking here, not just the homogeneous twenty-something crowds near the university. It seemed exotic, and though now I know the decor can be found in many of the city's Irish pubs, it was a long cry from the ubiquitous purple and gold, LSU-themed tiger shit pasted on the walls an hour away. We were totally charmed by the bar seats planted next to the window, which allowed you to enjoy both the show of the French Quarter's sidewalks and the affable crowd inside.

Even now, having made my way through our city's many Irish pubs, Molly's remains a favorite. The servers are always friendly, the long tables invite you to make new friends from across town or across the world. The frozen Irish coffee remains a treat on a hot New Orleans day.

The sign outside Molly's at the Market boasts that it is a "free house." Curious about the term, I asked a bartender to elaborate one night. Back in the nineteenth century, many bars were owned by either breweries or distilleries, which meant they could only serve the products produced by their respective owner. Free houses were just that: able to pour whatever the local publican wanted. The term also designated a place that wasn't beholden to a large company. This sensibility seems in keeping with the spirit of Molly's founder, Jim Monaghan, a man who once ran for City Council on the platform, "What the city needs is asses in seats." He was the instigator of two rowdy parades (one Carnival, one St. Paddy's Day) that continue to roll through the French Quarter. He was a man with a big personality who was never going to let anyone tell him how to live his life or run his bar. When you drink at Molly's, you can leave feeling a bit that you, too, can live your life like that. Jim's ashes lie behind the bar. Make sure to raise a toast.

NAPOLEON HOUSE

500 Chartres St. • (504) 524 9752
www.napoleonhouse.com
HOURS 11 a.m.–late (usually closes by midnight) Tue–Sat
NO HAPPY HOUR

I have given cocktail walking tours in the French Quarter since 2012. On these tours, we pass the Napoleon House. There are two observations people regularly make about the bar: "Wow, that place is awesome!" and "Wow, that place sure could use some work, or at least a coat of paint!" These comments, though they may seem in opposition, are really just two sides of the same coin. If you are in the second camp, you may want to skip the Napoleon House. What New Orleanians call "patina" you may call "disrepair." For us, the slightly crumbling facade of the bar speaks to two attributes New Orleanians prize: longevity and hospitality.

The Napoleon House was built in 1797 and was offered up by its owner as a refuge for the vanquished Emperor. He never came here, no matter what the buggy drivers may say. The only signs of Napoleon at the Napoleon House are a bust of the itty-bitty emperor behind the bar and a poster on the wall. The private home eventually became a grocery that served sandwiches. A bar in the back opened later. Joe Impastato ran the place in the 1950s, and it was under his tenure that the Pimm's Cup became the signature drink of the bar. I have two favorite drinking spots at the Napoleon House. In the front room, I always shoot for a table at the window. Its well-worn wood is smoothed down from the thousands of elbows that have polished it to a shine. If window seats are full, I'll see if there is seating in the spectacular yet intimate courtyard.

Regardless of where you sit, you'll be surrounded by the swelling sounds of opera and classical music, a welcome change from the 1980s cover bands on Bourbon Street just a few blocks away. The Napoleon House remained under the proprietorship of the Impastato family until 2015, when they turned the reins over to Ralph Brennan, of Brennan's Restaurant and

The historic Napoleon House with its beautful patina

Ralph's on the Park. When the torch passed from one family to another, there was hardly a peep among locals. For a town that doesn't handle change well, this is notable. But the Brennans are one of the few other families who can rival the Impastatos for longevity on the restaurant scene in New Orleans, and they seem to know what to do with this historic property, which is to not alter a damn thing.

OLD ABSINTHE HOUSE

240 Bourbon St. • (504) 523-3181
www.ruebourbon.com/oldabsinthehouse
HOURS 9 a.m.–2 a.m. Sun–Thu; 9 a.m.–4 a.m. Fri–Sat
NO HAPPY HOUR

The Old Absinthe House has been serving New Orleanians booze since 1806. Then, it was a grocery where you could buy wine and liquor. It later became Alex's Coffee House at a time when coffeehouses were a cross between saloons and places of business. Men would come to discuss the day's affairs and sip on coffee spiked with shots of brandy or whiskey. Privateer Jean Lafitte was supposed to have met here with General Andrew Jackson before the Battle of New Orleans, and the bar houses Jean Lafitte's Bistro in his honor. The coffeehouse later became The Absinthe Room, and aficionados of the Green Fairy would sit by bar's marble fountains, slowly dripping water over sugar cubes into their glasses of absinthe. The absinthe frappe, a popular nineteenth-century drink mixing absinthe and crushed ice, was allegedly invented and popularized here.

As for decor, the ceilings are covered with football helmets donated over the years by the very athletes that wore them on the field. The walls are covered with hundreds (thousands? millions?) of calling cards left by patrons over the years, and they have become as much a part of the bar's history as Jean Lafitte and the absinthe. As the bartender put it, "Taking even one down seems sacrilegious."

Depending on the time of day, the crowd at Old Absinthe House changes significantly. Its location on Bourbon Street means that it is often full of tourists late into the night. Mornings are slower, which means you have plenty of opportunity to chat with bartenders about the bar's history or have an eye opener if you were one of the aforementioned tourists. If you've never been to the Old Absinthe House, day-drinking here is a perfect introduction to its charms. As their slogan says, "Everyone you have known or ever will know eventually ends up at the Old Absinthe House." And don't forget to leave your card!

PALACE CAFE BLACK DUCK

605 Canal St. • (504) 523-1661
www.palacecafe.com
HOURS 10:30 a.m.–10 p.m. 7 days a week
HAPPY HOUR 4 p.m.–6 p.m. Mon–Fri

If the fourteen years of Prohibition in the United States were a joke, then New Orleans was the punch line. Federal agents dubbed it one of the wettest cities in the country. When the Feds sent most of their forces to shut down the drinking in New Orleans in 1926, they confiscated more than ten thousand cases of whiskey and champagne. Local bootleggers observed that the amount was so paltry a portion of their stockpile that the price wouldn't even be affected. When agent Isidore "Izzy" Einstein came to the city, it took him a mere thirty-five seconds to secure a drink compared to the lengthy fourteen minutes in New York. Of the many reasons it was easy to drink here, ready access to the Caribbean was an important one. Local smugglers had a short trip to the islands, which allowed access to both the rum produced there as well as the bounty of Europe's booze production. Boats zipped back and forth, hiding in the many inlets, bayous and swamps of the coast. The feds never had a chance. One such vessel was the Black Duck, a speedboat powered by twin Victory aircraft engines, faster than any U.S. Coast Guard craft. Though the boat primarily serviced the East Coast, it represents the many vessels that kept the thirsty nation well watered through The Great Mistake. The Black Duck Bar on the second floor at Dickie Brennan's Palace Café pays homage to the boat and its cargo, offering more than 130 rums for sipping.

As you ascend the beautiful Art Deco stairs, you leave behind the commercial bustle of Canal Street and sit above the fray at the gorgeous marble bar. Murals of famous New Orleans musicians surround you as you face a wall of rums. I am a big fan of using liquor as decoration, and it appears here to great effect. Who needs a menu when you can just scan the room? The Black Duck feels like an iconic New Orleans bar, with its slowly turning ceiling fans and well-togged staff, even though it is bigger than many bars in the French Quarter. It is definitely a place worth remembering if you are travelling in a group. The last time I was there, I sat among two separate bachelor/bachelorette parties. Each had commandeered a section of the bar, though after about an hour the two groups had begun to merge into a single unit.

The cocktails here range from good to outstanding, with Foster the People being one of my favorites. The rum flights are also a good place to start if you like your spirits neat. Fans of tequila will be pleased to see the nice selection offered here. There's a TV in the corner for those who want it, but it's unobtrusive and doesn't take away from this really lovely bar that feels old even though it just opened in 2015. The Black Duck is the beginning of what has become Rum Row. If you want to stay with the spirit, just meander on down to Tiki Tolteca and Latitude 29, ending at Cane & Table—all along the edge of the Quarter nearest the river—if you are still upright.

PAT O BRIEN'S

718 St. Peter St. • (504) 525-4823
www.patobriens.com
HOURS noon–til Mon–Thu; 10 a.m.–til Fri-Sun
NO HAPPY HOUR

The slogan at Pat O'Brien's is "Have fun!" It's an imperative most visitors don't need to hear. But if you are a local, it's nice to be reminded that this place where your parents and grandparents drank, where you came after prom, where you have ended up on so many nights, whether you wanted to or not, has always been here for you, to do just that.

If you come to New Orleans, you need to drink here. At least once and not ironically. Pat O'Brien's is an institution and for good reason. You will have a good time. Sober or inebriated (though the booze helps), alone or with company, Pat O'Brien's will sweep you along in a tide of revelry and celebration. They've been doing it since 1933 and they are professionals.

To start: Don't get a hurricane. You will want to. You are in the place where it was invented. You will feel an obligation. OK, buy one if you must,

Singing along to the tunes at Pat O'Brien's famed piano bar

but one only, to be split among your group. The drink is not good here. Perhaps it was, once, long ago in the 1940s, when wide-eyed GIs flooded the streets and everyone was singing "Rum and Coca Cola." Today it is a Kool-Aid–based concoction that tastes, if I may quote myself from another publication, "like chemical and disappointment." If you want a rum drink, order the rum punch, which is perfectly fine. Better yet, stick with a gin and tonic or a beer.

Next: Stake out territory on the patio. There's plenty of room and lots of turnover. Enjoy the changing colors of the fountain of fire. As you drink, the fountain will become even more impressive. After a round or two, you may tire of the raucous patio. That's OK. Pat O'Brien's offers plenty of spots to visit. You can pop into the side bar, adorned with hundreds of beer steins, which is usually fairly quiet. Stay there for a round if you like, then end your night in the piano bar. You will need to buy a round in here from one of the many waiters working the tables, but it is oh, so worth it.

Patrons sway to "Bobby McGee" and "Piano Man." You will know almost all the words to almost all the songs, and whether you are a singer or not, you will eventually find yourself raising your voice and your glass, joining in with the strangers who are now, for a moment, your comrades, joined together, having fun.

PIRATE'S ALLEY

622 Pirates Alley • (504) 524-9332
www.piratesalleycafe.com
HOURS noon–midnight Mon–Thu; 10 a.m.–midnight Fri–Sun
NO HAPPY HOUR

This little living room of a bar is located on the alley that connects Jackson Square to Royal Street. Named for the numerous smugglers and sellers of contraband who are alleged to have frequented the area, it was informally called "Pirate's Alley" long before the city formalized the street name in 1964. I know you are wondering, so yes, there's usually at least one pirate, whether behind the bar, or on a stool sipping a drink. Pirate paraphernalia covers the walls and if you sit with your back to the French doors, the space can feel a bit hokey, like you are in a bar adjacent to the Pirates of the Caribbean ride at Disney World. Instead, turn your gaze outward and enjoy the quiet view of the Cathedral. Though Jackson Square is often noisy, full of bands and tourists, this little strip alongside it is often tranquil, and the nook that is Pirate's Alley is the perfect spot to duck into between eating beignets and buying souvenir T-shirts. Absinthe fans can also taste an assortment of that spirit, poured by a knowledgeable staff.

Pirate's Alley Cafe is one of those French Quarter locations that is just as beloved by locals as it is by visitors. And whether your corset is tight or your tricorn hat is crooked, you will always be welcome.

SOBOU

310 Chartres St. • (504) 552-4095
www.sobounola.com
HOURS 6 a.m.–10 p.m. 7 days a week
HAPPY HOUR 3 p.m.–6 p.m.

SoBou, which stands for "South of Bourbon" is a direct nod to New York's Soho, NoLita and TriBeCa. This trend of compressing real estate markets into new words based on cardinal directions has travelled to other cities such as San Francisco and Austin. That trend didn't stick in New Orleans, mainly because north and south are hard to identify. When your city is between two bodies of water (Lake Pontchartrain and the Mississippi River), it's just easier to give directions in those terms. Though the name has lost its intended meaning, you should still go have a drink here.

SoBou is in the W, a hotel for the cool kids. The exposed beams and glass give it a sleek air. In lieu of candles or the Edison bulbs you see everywhere else, there is a softly lit glass square on one end of the granite bar, bathing drinkers in its warm light. It's a hip, modern bar in a hip, modern hotel, but thankfully the service offers nothing but old school New Orleans charm and hospitality.

Amiable Laura Bellucci oversees the cocktail program, which is not only delicious but maintains a bit of cheeky humor. In addition to pouring thoughtfully crafted beverages, the bar also serves one drink in an oversized flask like the kind you can buy on Bourbon Street. A large ice block is there for regular chiseling, and bartenders carve cubes to chill the several dozen

The modern look of SoBou's curving bar

rums, bourbons and scotches available for sampling. Since this is a hotel bar, you can count on a bartender who will just as happily make that Crown and Coke as she will your fifteen-ingredient craft libation, without an ounce of pretension. South of Bourbon, North of the River, drinking at SoBou is a lot of fun, no matter what direction you are headed.

SYLVAIN

625 Chartres St. • (504) 265-8123
www.sylvainnola.com
HOURS 5:30 p.m.–11 p.m. Mon–Thu; 10 a.m.–midnight Fri–Sat;
10:30 a.m.–10 p.m. Sun
NO HAPPY HOUR

Several years ago, I attended a bachelorette party in the French Quarter where I had the worst Manhattan of my life. As soon as I could politely excuse myself, I headed straight to Sylvain, where bartender Darren ameliorated my situation with a perfectly balanced Manhattan, served up. When I was looking at my notes on Sylvain for this book, I misread one of them. I had written "intentionally dark," but thought I had written "intellectually dark." Both are true. Sylvain is a moody little spot, dark and narrow. This experience begins with your arrival, which takes you down a narrow, dim, side alley into the space. There's not a lot of room in the bar for sitting or standing, and that intimacy and dim lighting make it a great place for a date. The decor is, well, odd, with unusual juxtapositions that make you cock your head in puzzlement. There's more taxidermy than makes sense, of wildlife that is definitely not local. Who shot that pheasant (named Almon-aster) perched above the back bar? Why hang a giant tattered American flag in a city that makes your forget you are in the United States at all? Best to not dwell on these matters, or you might lose your buzz. If there is no room at the bar, you can usually find a spot in the courtyard, which unlike the bar, feels about as New Orleans as it gets. None of the brick walls match each other, and the greenery is lush even in winter. But it's worth the wait if you can secure a stool inside, where you will be well taken care of by a staff that is very good at making delicious, slightly unusual drinks, including the Police

Offbeat decor at Sylvain

and Thieves with its dash of fir liqueur. Or you can just imbibe a Manhattan so lovely that it can wash away all the disappointing drinks you have ever had. Or, at least the ones you've had tonight.

TIKI TOLTECA

301 N. Peters St. • (504) 288-8226
www.tikitolteca.com
HOURS 5 p.m.–11 p.m. Mon–Thu; 3 p.m.–2 a.m. Fri and Sat; 3 p.m.–11 p.m. Sun
NO HAPPY HOUR

If I was a tiki fanatic, and had some money, the bar at Tiki Tolteca is the bar that I would build in my backyard. Bartenders work inside a hut with a thatched roof and bamboo poles adorned with tiki string lights. Roomy, leather-backed cane chairs circle a bar paneled with a woven grass facade. The rest of the room is dotted with similar leather chairs and tables, grouped into sections that make conversation easy. Large barrel-shaped rope and wicker lanterns illuminate the room. Easter Island statues line the walls, peering into the lively crowd.

If you visit, make sure to try your luck at the "Wheel of Fortune," where a $10 spin can either yield a well-priced MaïTai or the Escorpian Punch. Though you can order traditional tiki drinks here, Tiki Tolteca bartenders encourage you to try their specials. My favorite is the Columbus in Limbo, which comes with a postcard that the bar will mail for you. If the recipient brings the postcard to the bar, they get a free drink. (And, yes, they do put it in the mail. I've sent several and they all made it to their destinations, despite their slightly illegible addresses.) In 2014, Tiki Tolteca was named *Food & Wine* magazine's People's Choice Best New Bar in the U.S. Though I haven't visited all the nominees, Tiki Tolteca certainly holds its own as the kind of place you wish you had in your backyard.

TUJAGUE'S

823 Decatur St. • (504) 525 8676
www.tujaguesrestaurant.com
HOURS 11 a.m.–10 p.m. 7 days a week
NO HAPPY HOUR

In the mid-nineteenth century, the French Quarter was a working-class neighborhood, filled with immigrants who sold their wares at the French Market. Work started before dawn and ended midday when the market closed. Back then, your main meal was taken around 2 p.m., which is a long time to wait to eat when your previous refreshment was breakfast before sunrise. A savvy butcher's wife, Elizabeth Kettering Begue, decided to start

A bartender pours a milk punch at Tujagues

Ann Tunnerman

Ann Tunnerman worked in New Orleans radio and television marketing for much of her professional life, but she found her passion when she created a cocktail tour of the French Quarter in 2001. To celebrate the first anniversary of her business, she invited notable cocktail aficionados to come and speak about cocktail history and dubbed the event Tales of the Cocktail. People had such a good time, they asked her to do it again. Since then, Tales (as locals call it) has grown to be one of the largest spirits industry conferences in the United States, bringing bartenders, tastemakers and brand representatives to New Orleans each summer. What started as an afternoon affair has become a weeklong celebration of the power of spirits.

Ann's original goal may have been to highlight the importance of the New Orleans cocktail scene, but the effects of Tales exceed merely honoring the city's drinking legacy. The economic impact of the event on New Orleans is considerable. It lures thousands of participants and has generated millions of dollars, both of which are especially valued coming in the summer, when tourism is slow. But more importantly, Tales has directly and indirectly changed drinking in New Orleans.

As Neal Bodenheimer, proprietor of Cure, observed, "I don't think Cure could exist without Ann. I wouldn't have found so many like-minded people to staff the bar if she hadn't stirred up the community." Local bartender Kimberly Patton-Bragg notes that Tales is a resource for bartenders across the country who find out what folks are up to in other regions. "We learn about cool products, new techniques, how to save space behind the bar," she says. "Without Tales, you wouldn't have these kinds of cocktail programs in other cities."

Ann is just as proud of her impact on the national scene as she is of her local achievements. Tales has facilitated the launch of two cocktail-based companies: El Guapo Bitters and Cocktail & Sons Syrups. Ann remembers that when she first approached El Guapo owner Scot Mattox about selling his bitters at the Tales Bitters Market, he was surprised. Though he had been making his own bitters for some time, it had never even occurred to him to turn it into a business. Now he sells his products through Amazon and distributes them across the globe. Max Messier received similar encouragement for his line of cocktail syrups. Ann is enthusiastic about both of these brands—not only do their flavors reflect southern Louisiana, both companies are based here. In the past they might have had to leave the state to succeed, but not anymore. Ann feels that Tales has helped lay the groundwork in this town to support these kinds of businesses and that it gives locals an international market in which to pitch their spirits products. As she says, "I always want Tales of the Cocktail to be a bloodline back to New Orleans. When I started I didn't intend to change the industry; I just wanted people to understand our stories."

Ann has also tried to give back to the industry. Tales of the Cocktail is actually a non-profit, and it has supported bartenders with tuition reimbursements for classes that help them run their business as well as offering a medical fund if someone needs a hand with bills or support while recovering from an injury. "People don't realize that we are paying it forward, being good to the people who are good to us," Ann says. "I like being able to help people out."

Tales of the Cocktail is entering its fourteenth year and has expanded its reach with traveling conferences around the world. But at its core, it is still a locally created event. Ann hopes it becomes her legacy, her gift, to the city.

offering full meals to the hungry workers when their shift ended, and in doing so, she created the concept of brunch. In 1863, she opened her restaurant in what is now Tujague's and called it Begue's. In 1865, the Tujague family opened a restaurant just a few doors down from the formidable Madame Begue. After her death in the early twentieth century, they bought the property from her daughter and moved their restaurant into its current spot. So while the restaurant has been in business for 160 years, it has done so in two different locations.

Tujague's bar is the oldest stand-up bar in New Orleans, and no, that doesn't mean they do comedy there. In the past, many bars did not offer seating, instead running a brass rail under the bar on which men could rest a foot. Once you know that is how bars used to be built, you start to see that style everywhere. You can tell if a wooden bar was built during that era because there's no lip for a stool to scoot under. Stand-up bars tended to cater to a more working-class patron who didn't need fancy seats. The bar here is actually older than the restaurant, brought over from France to New Orleans in 1856 and ensconced in the building years later. Its polished sheen is only exceeded by the shine of the mirror behind the bar.

Tujague's still retains its roots as a place where men packed in to have a few drinks after a long day, and though there are two tables where you can sit, this is still a bar where most folks stand to drink. Bartender Richard Odell enjoys working behind the stick at a place without stools. When people sit, he notes, they are planted and often prevent others from accessing him. If everyone is standing, there is an easy give and take, and people don't feel like they have their own special spot they have to protect.

It's good to have this method of crowd control in place. Tujague's receives a steady stream of drinkers, some who have stopped in because of its storied past, others merely because it's the closest door that's open. One minute Odell can be pouring a whiskey and Coke, another he can be mixing up the bar's signature drink, the Grasshopper. If you do order one, make sure to toast the portrait of the man in the white linen suit who surveys the bar. That's Philbert Guichet, the man who invented the drink. Once you've tried the Grasshopper, it's time to move on to other classics. Though Odell says he's equally happy to make a highball as he is to make something more complicated, you owe it to yourself to order one of the standards here and place your foot where countless men and women have rested theirs while they raised their glasses to a long day's work, done well and now, done.

THE VOODOO

718 N. Rampart St. • (504) 265-0953
www.facebook.com/The-Voodoo-Lounge
HOURS 24 hours a day 7 days a week
NO HAPPY HOUR

Back in 2009, I had a roommate who worked the graveyard shift at the Voodoo, and I would often pop in for a drink to keep him company. Back then, the clientele at the Voodoo were either filled with cocaine or despair or both. In 2015, the folks who ran Flanagan's, one of my favorite French Quarter neighborhood bars, lost their lease and were looking for new digs. They took over the Voodoo and brought with them their ability to run a 24-hour joint that still manages to keep things friendly and easygoing, even at four in the morning. Bartender Houla told me that when they re-opened under this new ownership, a few of the former Voodoo patrons came looking to engage their "regular activities," but once they learned that they couldn't do blow on the bar or get a blowjob in the back, they left the bar to Flanagan's fans and anyone looking for a friendly, late-night spot.

Compared to many 24-hour joints, the Voodoo has a stellar whiskey selection, including many high-end scotches. I bought Lee a pour of Ardbeg, not cheap, but a nice treat at the end of a night. Houla and I got to talking about Flanagan's, and I told him about its entry in my other book, *The French Quarter Drinking Companion*. One memorable night at Flanagan's, I overheard a conversation between two guys behind the bar in which one lamented the difficulty of replicating his mother's banana bread recipe. The juxtaposition of two beefy, inked-up guys commiserating about failed banana bread was too charming for me to leave out of the book. Houla's eyes widened when I told him this story. "That was me!" he exclaimed. We spent the rest of the night reminiscing about good times at Flanagan's, as well as discussing plans for the good times to come at the Voodoo. It was a typical New Orleans night, when you run into the friend you just met.

ALGIERS

CROWN AND ANCHOR

200 Pelican Ave. • (504) 227-1007
crownandanchor.pub
HOURS 11 a.m.–4 a.m. (or as long as people are in the bar)
HAPPY HOUR 4 p.m.–7 p.m. Mon–Fri

The British were defeated at the Battle of New Orleans in 1815, but if they had managed to make it up the river, they would have found a patch of home at the Crown and Anchor. Located across the river from the French Quarter at the foot of the Algiers ferry landing, the Crown and Anchor is a charming British pub with all the coziness of an old seaport tavern. Step through the blue British police callbox into a space with low lights and a lower ceiling. Scores of pint glasses hang above your head, and nautical-themed decor lines the walls. The taps pour British favorites: Guinness, of course, as well as Bass, Fuller's London Porter, and Blackthorn Hard Cider. English beer bar towels are set along the bar like placemats and serve as oversized coasters. I overheard the bartender explain to a customer that the Crown and Anchor Bar was a traditional British pub and poured Imperial pints. When asked what an Imperial pint was, she explained that it meant the pint glasses held twenty ounces instead of sixteen. Some quick googling revealed the origin of this standard: the British Weights and Measures Act of 1824. This act fixed measurements across the kingdom and, in doing so, set the size of a glass of beer there. The United States continued to use an older measurement that set a pint at sixteen ounces. But since British pubs continue to use the twenty-ounce measurement, the Crown and Anchor follows their lead.

The Crown and Anchor is a friendly local spot. The bar fills up on Thursday trivia nights, the hardest in town, according to Lee. But most of the time regulars drift in and out, greeting the bartender with familiar smiles. The Crown and Anchor is worth a visit, especially if doing so gets you on the ferry, which affords a wonderful view of the French Quarter from the Mississippi River.

OLD POINT BAR

545 Patterson Dr. • (504) 364-0950
www.oldpointbarnola.com
HOURS 11 a.m.–4 or 5 a.m.
NO HAPPY HOUR

The Old Point Bar has appeared in over forty movies, including *Green Lantern*, the Oscar-winning *Ray*, Sylvester Stallone's *The Expendables*, and Nicolas Cage's *Seeking Justice*. And there's good reason, too. Its worn, wooden floors and walls exude a palpable feeling of age. A lot of people have passed a lot of time in this space. In the nineteenth century, the Old Point was a coffeehouse, back when coffeehouses served as much brandy as they did coffee. It later became a music spot, popular among African American musicians who were not welcome in many white clubs in New Orleans. Now everyone is welcome here, and you can catch a variety of musical acts pretty much any night of the week.

There's just enough quirky decor to keep the place from feeling like a movie set. Lovely carved mermaid figureheads, loosed from their ships and attached near the ceiling, keep watch above the patrons. They rest among scores of license plates that pepper the walls. It's a relaxed, comfortable bar with low prices and a set of patrons who know each other and who call the bartenders by name. The Old Point embodies what is charming about Algiers. It feels like New Orleans because it is New Orleans, but the pace also feels a little slower than the rest of the city. Things are a little more laid back on this side of the river.

CHAPTER 2

Bywater and the Marigny

Just down the Mississippi River from the French Quarter lies the Marigny. It's named for Jean-Bernard Xavier Philippe de Marigny de Mandeville, better known as Bernard Marigny, who owned the plantation from which this neighborhood was carved. Bernard was a bon vivant who allegedly introduced the dice game craps to the citizens of New Orleans. Despite his fondness for the game, he was apparently terrible at it, and over time he gambled most of his wealth away. Marigny eventually decided to sell the land to the city, but before doing so he carved the plantation into streets, naming them as he went along. Notably, the street now called Burgundy was originally Rue de Craps, a nod to his favorite pastime. By the early 1800s, his plantation was owned by the city.

The next neighborhood down the river is the Bywater, separated from the Marigny by the train tracks at Press Street. This area was a staging ground for many of the troops who fought in the Battle of New Orleans just down the Mississippi River in Chalmette. The British were defeated there under the leadership of Andrew Jackson, whose statue graces Jackson Square in the French Quarter. Both the Marigny and the Bywater were working-class neighborhoods throughout the nineteenth and early twentieth century. Their proximity to the port made them popular among people who worked on the wharf. In recent years, the neighborhoods have become popular among young millennials, so instead of salty sea captains drinking rum in taverns, you will see coffeehouses full of guys in skinny pants and Warby Parker glasses. Tennessee Williams set his play *A Streetcar Named Desire* in the Marigny near Elysian Fields, and the Desire Streetcar to which he refers ran along Desire Street, which sits four blocks from the train tracks in the Bywater.

Bywater

BACCHANAL

600 Poland Ave. • (504) 948-9111

www.bacchanalwine.com

HOURS 11 a.m.–midnight 7 days a week

HAPPY HOUR 11 a.m.–6 p.m.

Bacchanal started as a hole in the wall, one-room wine shop at the corner of Poland and Chartres. It opened when the Bywater neighborhood was charming and dingy. Nothing much was around, except a military base—not exactly a wine crowd. I was surprised when it opened and wondered how long it would stay in business. Living a few blocks away, I did my part to ensure its longevity. Today, Bacchanal is a massive complex, featuring a sprawling patio, upstairs bar, and first-rate kitchen. The story of Bacchanal is, in a way, a snapshot of my neighborhood after Katrina.

Chris Rudge, the owner, was a generous, affable proprietor, full of advice, always happy to share tastings and stories. He didn't take himself (or wine) too seriously. He used to sell a bottle of Aubry Rose champagne with a guarantee that if you drank it with the object of your affection, you would get laid, and if you didn't, you could bring the empty bottle back for a refund. Apparently no one ever returned with an empty, and I'm not telling what happened after I shared a bottle.

After Hurricane Katrina, when the levees failed and the city flooded, many local restaurants remained shuttered, and the closest open grocery store was seven miles away. But Bacchanal quickly reopened, and Chris offered his place to a local chef who cooked on a grill in his pickup truck parked on the patio. Truthfully, "patio" is a generous term for the gravelly concrete slab where we sat on rickety broken plastic chairs, balancing good food on paper plates on our knees and worrying about the future of our city. The wine helped.

The popularity of the patio grew, musicians began to perform on a regular basis, the kitchen thrived, and Bacchanal became a hub of community activity. Eventually neighbors alerted the city to the fact that Chris didn't have a permit for anything besides selling and pouring wine. What was once a small wine shop had become a nuisance, and the city shut all of these other activities down. But instead of returning to being merely a wine store, Chris built out a proper kitchen adjacent to a beautifully renovated courtyard and got all the permits needed to become a venue. He later added an enclosed bar above the shop, where patrons dash during inclement weather.

The Bacchanal you visit today is far removed from the one where I first bought wine in 2004. The patio is the main attraction. Folks drink wine under Christmas lights and listen to live music. The kitchen is inventive and reliable. The wine prices have definitely gone up, and buying a bottle there is akin to buying one in a restaurant instead of a shop, but a restaurant/venue is what Bacchanal has become. Weekend nights can get crowded, and the local in me rolls her eyes at the lines of people elbowing their way to secure a table. But when I feel myself getting cranky, I remind myself that not that long ago, we wondered if anyone would ever come drink here again, and I get over my impatience. Chris died in his sleep in 2015, and those of us who had been his customers have mourned that loss. I know he was proud of what he created. Bacchanal is not the intimate neighborhood secret it was in 2004, but it still offers a true New Orleans experience of good food, wine, and music under the stars.

BUD RIP'S

900 Piety St. • (504) 945-5762
No website
HOURS 1 p.m.–til 7 days a week
NO HAPPY HOUR

Bud Rip's has no sign. But local bars don't need signs. If you aren't sure you are in the right place, look for the name laid out in tile on the front stoop. Bud Rip was a New Orleans political figure in the 1950s and 1960s; his photo hangs above the bar in tribute. For many years, the patrons of Bud Rip's looked about the right age to have voted for the bar's namesake, but as the neighborhood has changed, so has the crowd, and now you find guys in skinny pants and Warby Parker frames drinking alongside Ninth Ward regulars. The folks who own the R Bar, another favorite watering hole in the Marigny Triangle, recently took over the bar, and their presence is palpable in an improved beer list and bartenders who can make a decent Old Fashioned if you are in the mood for fancy. During football games, patrons turn the day into a potluck, and in addition to your very reasonably priced beer, you can make a plate of beans and rice, potato salad, and brownies. Come for the pressed-tin ceiling and stay for the weathered New Orleans political photos and posters. It seems like every time I go to Bud Rip's, someone is having a birthday. It doesn't matter if you know the birthday honoree or not; you'll still get cake.

JUNCTION

3021 St. Claude Ave. • (504) 272-0205
www.junctionnola.com
HOURS 11 a.m.–2 a.m. 7 days a week
NO HAPPY HOUR

Aptly located near the train tracks separating the Marigny from the Bywater, Junction was opened in 2015 by the same folks who own Molly's at the Market in the French Quarter, a team that knows a thing or two about running a welcoming neighborhood bar. Railway prints and schedules adorn the walls, and the vibe is slightly railway depot, especially when the train passes and blows its horn. Junction features forty taps and specializes in Louisiana craft beers as well as those from breweries in Mississippi and Alabama. I love the beer menu at Junction: a plastic flip-chart with a graphic for each beer and a detailed explanation of its style and flavor. Though the focus here is on beer, the liquor selection, though small, offers enough choices to make a whiskey fan happy. Junction does a mean burger, as attested to by the steady stream of customers picking up to-go orders.

The bar fills up during their regular "Meet the Brewer" nights and when it screens classic flicks ranging from *The Shining* to *King Creole*. Also, I'm a total sucker for Junction's walk-up window, where you can hang on the sidewalk with your smoker friends and never have to elbow your way to the bar to get a drink. Junction is a great spot for sampling Louisiana brews among locals.

MARKEY'S BAR

640 Louisa St. • (504) 943-0785
www.facebook.com/MarkeysBarNOLA
HOURS 11 a.m.–3 a.m. 7 days a week
NO HAPPY HOUR

Originally a riverfront bar catering to dock workers (they opened at 6 a.m. and closed at 10 p.m.), Markey's transitioned to more traditional hours when the nearby wharves closed in the 1970s. It passed from Joe Markey, who opened it in 1947, to his son, Roy Markey Sr., who handed it to current owner, Roy Markey Jr. A good friend of mine, Steven Forster, told me a story about what Markey's was like in the 1960s, when it still catered to the dockworkers crowd. Steven grew up in the neighborhood, and one day when he was about sixteen, he accompanied his father to Markey's where he was meeting up with some friends. Steven stressed to me that his father was a very upright person who never cursed. Before they entered Markey's, Steven's dad turned to him and said, "You are going to hear the word 'fuck' in here." And he sure did.

Not much has changed in that regard, though the clientele now features more baristas and artists and fewer blue-collar workers. Markey's is Lee's favorite neighborhood bar, and he has watched it change over the last eight years with interest. He approves of the added beer taps and the decent bar food but bemoans the absence of $2.50 High Life, no longer on draft but only available in a bottle. For me, the bar feels much the same as it did when I moved to the Bywater in 2003. I usually run into someone I know, and the crowd feels full of locals. Tourists aren't making the trek to Markey's. Bar owner Roy agrees that Markey's remains a true neighborhood bar. He told me that when the bar reopened after Katrina, people would leave notes taped to the building, letting friends know they were OK and seeking out loved ones whom they had not heard from. In the aftermath of disaster, people came to a bar looking for each other. Markey's still feels like a place where that could happen. It doesn't get any more New Orleans than that.

N7

1117 Montegut St. • No Phone
No website
HOURS 6 p.m.–10 p.m. Mon–Sat
NO HAPPY HOUR

Route Nationale 7, or "N7," was France's version of Route 66, a mythical road that defined summer for generations of French families. In the 1950s and '60s, the road was known as "La Route des Vacances" or "The Holiday Route," as middle-class workers drove their new (affordable) Citroëns

A slice of southern France at N7

to vacation in southern France and Italy. Small farmhouses along the route were converted to informal restaurants, offering simple fare to travelling families, as well as to truckers who drove the road throughout the year. Soon the Michelin tire company assembled a list of these venues, and from that was born the venerated Michelin guide.

The bar N7 recreates this farmhouse experience, but you only have to travel a bit down St. Claude Avenue to get there. Their sign is discreet, just a red stenciled logo on the gate of a fence, but once you open that gate, you leave New Orleans and enter the French countryside. N7 is utterly charming. A beat-up Citroën is parked outside the small wooden building that houses a tiny bar and mismatched wooden tables. A covered patio beckons when the weather is cooler, and even on a sultry night, there are patrons enjoying bottles of wine there. Inside, the soundtrack is decidedly international, and French movie posters and magazine covers paper the walls. But what adds to the feeling that you have left the city is not so much the decor as the architecture itself. They got the windows right: small, multi-paned affairs that you don't see in New Orleans. The low ceiling is a stark contrast to the lofty affairs found in most buildings in this neighborhood.

N7 is officially licensed as a wine bar, and the bulk of their list comprises French wines, augmented by other international varieties. There is a small but carefully curated beer list (even the draft beers are French!) and a tiny bar with an abundant selection of vermouths and aperitifs. The menu is also small and, interestingly, features a number of imported canned treats: pâté, smoked trout, octopus in ink, as well as duck à l'orange and, occasionally, vichyssoise. The food prices are on the high side, but you can drink here very reasonably, with bottles under $25 and glasses that start at $7.

The bar's namesake road is no longer called N7. It is now Departmentale 6007, a demotion of sorts that signifies the road's secondary status—there are far faster ways to get from Paris to the south of France. But its spirit lives on in a quiet section of the Bywater.

OXALIS

3162 Dauphine St. • (504) 267-4776
oxalisbywater.com
HOURS 4 p.m.–11 p.m Mon–Fri; 5 p.m.–11 p.m. Sat and Sun
The Branch bar 7 p.m.–2 a.m. Fri and Sat
HAPPY HOUR 4 p.m.–7 p.m. Mon–Fri
When you walk in, tell 'em you want to sit in outside on the patio. In order to get a table on the patio, you may have to get food, so when they ask if you are eating, say yes and then at least get some fries so you aren't a liar. Oxalis's interior is fine, but it's the multiple courtyards that keep me spending my money on their very reasonably priced, very well made cocktails. The first

courtyard (the big one, open every day) has the usual New Orleans court-yard accoutrements: chipped walls with plants growing on and out of them, some intentionally, some not. The patio furniture looks like something you might have in your yard: black iron tables and chairs, with a long table near the back wall that seats larger parties. Drinking here midweek is casual and easy amid the quiet of the courtyard. It's lovely no matter what night you come, but if you can, try to have a drink there on a weekend. That's when Oxalis opens The Branch, a hidden nook of a bar and courtyard, located

A nice glass of red at N7

behind the larger courtyard. The bar seats five on a good day, and unless it is very early or very late, you shouldn't plan to linger. People will be constantly elbowing through you to order their drinks. Instead, grab your cocktail and head out to the oasis in back. On rare chilly nights, sit by the fire or wear a coat. Otherwise, grab a chair by the fountain. I don't know why more people aren't drinking here on the weekend in this tucked-away piece of heaven, especially when the drinks are always solid no matter who is doing the mixing. I often order my way around the specials, but no matter what, my first drink here (and often my second or third) is their signature Old Fashioned. Five dollars, people. Six bucks for a nice pour of whiskey, not too sweet, with just enough bitters. A paltry rent in so lovely a locale.

SATURN BAR

3067 St. Claude Ave. • (504) 949-7532
www.saturnbar.com
HOURS 5 p.m.–til Mon–Sat; 6 p.m.–til Sun
Their website states: Sometimes we open at random times, so if you see the neon lights on outside, it means come on in.
NO HAPPY HOUR

There is so much to see at the Saturn Bar. Paintings of bullfighters, bayou scenes, saints, and sinners cover the dusty wooden walls. The Saturn Bar is dark, and everyone likes it that way. Even the neon signs on the wall can't overcome the dimness. If you just came here to drink, then you'll probably stay in the front room, chatting with the bartender or locals. If you came for a show, head to the back and go upstairs to what Lee calls "the boxing ring." Here a balcony encircles the "stage" (read: ground floor) and you can peer down on acts below. It feels like you should be betting on an illegal fighting match of some kind, but instead you get to witness local music acts, movie nights, mod dance parties, or some combination thereof.

The Saturn Bar has been a favorite local hangout since 1961, when O'Neil Broyard took it over. Back then, the Ninth Ward was a working-class neighborhood, and the bar catered to locals. One of those locals was Mike Frolich, whom Broyard had known from childhood. Frolich volunteered to paint the ceiling, and Broyard acquiesced. As Broyard said in an interview before his death, "We built a scaffold and Mike went to pick up some paint and rollers. You know, it was just like out of Michelangelo." When Frolich finished, he offered to continue his decorating. Broyard bought him paint and brushes, and over the next few years Frolich created a series of murals. As Broyard observed, "One day I add up all the slips and it turns out I'd spent $1,800 on all that stuff."

The murals are amazing, and if there's enough light, you should grab your drink and take a tour around this unusual gallery. There's one painting honoring the discovery of the New World, complete with the *Niña*, *Pinta*, and *Santa Maria*. Another explores the cosmos, with the earth, the sun, and a rocket ship heading to the moon. The painting of St. Bernadette giving a rose to Fatima was made for Broyard's mother. If you can tear your eyes away from the fantastic scenes above, you might notice a giant turtle hanging on the wall, bearing the word "Candy" on his shell. You know how some bars are dog friendly? The Saturn Bar was turtle friendly. Broyard acquired the live turtle from a seafood truck, and it lived in the bar for some time as a kind of mascot. When the turtle died, Broyard had him stuffed and mounted. Why "Candy?" It was a nod to Broyard's motto in his former life, when he was a bookie. When gamblers would lose, he would tell them, "It's like taking candy from a baby."

Broyard died in December 2005, but his family took up the mantle of running the bar. Of course, some things changed. If you can believe it, they actually removed a great deal of the clutter and left behind just enough tchotchkes, trinkets, and memorabilia to keep it feeling familiar. They now welcome a robust lineup of bands who perform most evenings, and the crowd has expanded beyond the old-timers who had been drinking here since Broyard opened up. But the Saturn Bar still feels like a place that has been around for a long time, and its cheap drinks and local vibe remain.

VAUGHN'S

4229 Dauphine St. • (504) 947-5562
https://www.facebook.com/Vaughans-Lounge
HOURS noon–til 7 days a week
NO HAPPY HOUR
Cash only

Vaughn's has always been on my short list of favorite places to watch a Saints game; it's a stone's throw from my house, with a rowdy home crowd equally prepared to cheer when the Saints win or have another round to commiserate after a loss. It's a neighborhood joint that celebrates its musical heritage, decorated with both beer signs and photographs of New Orleans musicians. Most visitors to New Orleans know it as the music venue in the HBO show *Treme*. Even before that show, word about this great neighborhood joint being a cool spot to visit had made its way to folks in the know. The wooden floor has plenty of room for dancing, and the long bar readily accommodates the dozens of folks who come for regular, late-night music gigs. During music breaks, weary dancers take a rest on the benches that line the outside walls. When summer showers arrive, you can stay protected under the slightly sagging overhang, the rain making its own kind of music.

The Marigny

THE ALLWAYS LOUNGE AND THEATER

2240 St. Claude Ave. • (504) 218-5778
www.theallwayslounge.net
HOURS 6 p.m.–late Tue–Sun
NO HAPPY HOUR

You never know exactly what you're going to get at the AllWays, but you can be sure you will have a good time getting it. Sundays are swing nights, when Lindy Hoppers from across the city come to dance to a rotating set of jazz bands. Thursdays (my favorites) feature Drag Bingo. There's regular burlesque and the occasional cat circus coming through the doors as well. All find the spotlight on a velvet-curtained stage that leaves plenty of room for folks to groove—or at least sway—on the dance floor. If you don't want to dance, you can find a spot at the many high-top tables that line the walls or take a seat at the curving red and black bar, where a friendly staff pours a generous serving of well whiskey for $4. If you are flush, you can try one of their signature cocktails. There's a Prohibition-era Bee's Knees for the swing set and a Chartreuse-laced Wig Snatcher for those in drag. The red walls give the room a turn of the century bordello charm and the two(!) disco balls keep everyone in a party mood. Whatever you order and whenever you go, the AllWays is a bright spot on the new, hip, St. Claude strip.

BUFFA'S

1001 Esplanade Ave. • (504) 949-0038

www.buffasbar.com

HOURS 24 hours a day, 7 days a week

HAPPY HOUR 4 a.m.–6 a.m. and 4 p.m.–6 p.m.

Buffa's is a beloved neighborhood spot perched on the edge of the French Quarter. I used to live a block away and spent many an afternoon day drinking among locals, some of whom seemed to have been sitting on their stools since the bar opened in 1939. Buffa's bartenders are friendly souls who pour a strong gin and tonic, and even during the madness of Mardi Gras when the bar is packed, they remain calm and affable. Buffa's decor is your standard "old-timers neighborhood bar," heavy on neon beer signs and poker machines. The terrazzo floor and pressed-tin ceiling are lovely touches, best appreciated if you are drinking in daylight when the sun pours through the unusual, pill-shaped windows. Despite its proximity to the Quarter, the bar never feels touristy, with the balance of patrons tipped toward folks who live nearby instead of those wearing out-of-season Mardi Gras beads or T-shirts that say "I got Bourbon faced on Shit Street." Make your way to the back room of the bar to hear live music most nights of the week.

D.B.A.

618 Frenchmen St. • No phone number

www.dbaneworleans.com

HOURS 5 p.m.–til Mon–Thur; 4 p.m.–til Fri–Sun

NO HAPPY HOUR

D.B.A. is one of the more popular music venues on Frenchmen Street, but it merits a mention in this book because it also has the best whiskey and beer list on that stretch. In addition to their twenty taps, you'll find an extensive bottle list, broken down by country on their menu board. Their whiskey selection is equally robust. Dozens of American bourbons nestle next to their Scotch and Irish cousins behind the bar. At D.B.A. you can sip on Elijah Craig or splurge on some Lagavulin. While you can certainly get that PBR and a shot here, D.B.A. is a classy enough spot that you might want to up your game.

One reason I really enjoy going to D.B.A. to hear music is because the layout of the bar allows you to choose your level of participation in the show. D.B.A. is split into two connecting rooms, and the wall that divides these spaces is wrapped by the bar itself. In one room you'll find the venue, and in the other you'll find a more traditional bar. If you plant yourself on the latter side, you can still hear the music (especially if it is a brass band) but you can also have a conversation. I tend to bounce back and forth between the two sides throughout the night, happy to be able to hear both my friends and the bands with ease.

HI HO

2239 St. Claude Ave. • (504) 945-4446
HOURS 5 p.m.–2 a.m. Sun–Thu; 5 p.m.–4 a.m. Fri and Sat
HAPPY HOUR 5 p.m.–8 p.m.

In late 2008, I got laid off. I now refer to 2009 as "The Lost Year"—I went on unemployment, drank heavily, and dated a musician. I did much of that drinking at the Hi Ho. It was pretty close to my house and the drinks were cheap, but I also liked it because there was usually music playing, and there wasn't a cover. I particularly enjoyed sipping a beer on Mondays during the bluegrass jam session. It's hard to feel despair around banjos. By 2010, I had started to get my life back in order, and there were fewer nights at the Hi Ho.

Like much of New Orleans in the last six years, some things have changed and some have stayed remarkably the same. For one, the Hi Ho now has a cocktail menu, created in response to the many tourists who have been making their way to the bar from Frenchmen Street. When I tried to order one of these new potions, the bartender passed my order to the other bartender, Dallas, who is apparently "the cocktail guy." Dallas has worked all over the bar scene in New Orleans, from strip clubs to high-end craft cocktail joints, but he prefers the Hi Ho because he likes the clientele and the laid-back vibe. That's one thing that hasn't changed here. The decor of the bar has also remained informal and quirky. The mirror behind the back bar is covered with multicolored paper signs, most affixed with scotch tape, promoting drink specials, movie nights and upcoming acts. There's still a lot of bathroom graffiti, always a sign of a good neighborhood bar. Favorite passages include: "Have selfish love," "Emma Jane loves Lexi to the moon and back," "Life does not have to be perfect to be beautiful." In a town where so many bars sport a highly manicured look, it's comforting to be able to order a $3 PBR in a place where nothing matches.

The back patio is new and nicely tricked-out. A mural combining Mexican wrestlers and Fidel Castro does not have to make sense in order to be remarkable. The bar's kitchen, Fry & Pie, is located on the patio and serves late. Yes, they only serve french fries with various sauces/toppings and mini sweet pies, and, yes, they are both delicious. If you need to be entertained, this is a joint with a lot of "programming." Friday nights feature '80s movies with free Nintendo, and there are comedy acts on the weekends. But it's also the kind of place where you can just keep ordering your cheap beers and whiskey shots from Dallas while talking to the moon and back with your friends all night.

KAJUN'S

2256 St. Claude Ave. • (504) 947-3735
www.kajunpub.com
HOURS 24 hours a day, 7 days a week
HAPPY HOUR 7 a.m.–7 p.m. 7 days a week

Kajun's bartender Chris Wecklein once told me, "Everyone loves to sing." As someone who has worked Kajun's daily karaoke for three years, he ought to know. The fun starts each day at 5 p.m. until no one wants to sing or drink anymore. As you can imagine, the singing often ends late at this divey spot. It's hard to leave a place where you can combine your love of belting out Journey or Taylor Swift with $7 PBR pitchers. The "777" happy hour (7 a.m.–7 p.m., 7 days a week) and Jell-O shots keep everyone's voices lubricated and nerves fortified. It doesn't matter what kind of singer you are; everyone gets a cheer at Kajun's.

Locals also know the bar's owner, JoAnn, as one of the people profiled in the book *Nine Lives* and the musical it inspired, both of which followed the paths of nine New Orleanians from Hurricane Betsy through Hurricane Katrina. You can buy copies of the book or CD in the vending machine near the back of the bar, and if JoAnn is there, she will happily sign them. Chris sang on the CD, so make sure to get his signature as well. If you are just starting your night, the vending machine also provides cigarettes, beef jerky,

Altoids and Advil. No matter what kind of night/morning awaits you, you can always leave Kajun's prepared.

LOST LOVE LOUNGE

2529 Dauphine St. • (504) 949-2009
www.facebook.com/LostLoveLounge
HOURS 4 p.m.–1 a.m, or possibly 2 a.m. Mon–Sat
HAPPY HOUR 4 p.m.–7 p.m.

A lot of bars act as de facto community centers, but at least once a year, Lost Love Lounge is kind of an official one. March 19, Saint Joseph's Day, is a big day on the New Orleans Catholic calendar. Though the festivities may not match those for St. Patrick, many churches in New Orleans create enormous altars to the saint. Church members bake special cakes and breads shaped like the tools St. Joseph used. The altars are assembled a few days before, and then they are taken apart on the feast day and used to feed the hungry. These altars abound all over New Orleans; even our local grocery store, Rouse's, has one. But my favorite St. Joseph altar is at the Lost Love Lounge. Patrons from all over the neighborhood bring pasta, stuffed artichokes, seafood and other bounty and serve it all under a disco ball. It's usually the one day of the year I'm drinking there in daylight.

I love how much of a manifestation of the neighborhood the festival is, because the bar is just as welcoming on the other 364 days of the year. The Lost Love Lounge is a little hipster, a little divey. The furniture is scruffy, from the dilapidated sofa to bar stools that all show quite a bit of wear, even in the dark. It's the only bar I know of with a lending library. The drinks, including a decent beer list, are well priced. There isn't a cocktail menu per se, but several popular mixed drinks, including Dark and Stormys, Pimm's Cups, and Bloody Marys, are on offer. The programming features comedy shows, the occasional bit of live music, and AMC and HBO shows, among other things. NB: if you plan to drink here during popular shows (e.g., *Game of Thrones*), you may be shushed by the crowd, and too bad if you aren't a fan. But the bar is good about posting a sign reminding you of the schedule. If you arrive during a show, just walk down the block to Mimi's, kill an hour and return.

THE MAYHAW

2381 St. Claude Ave. • (504) 609-3813
www.strochmarket.com
HOURS 7 a.m.–9 p.m. Sun–Thu; 7 a.m.–11 p.m. Fri and Sat
HAPPY HOUR 4 p.m.–6 p.m.

Throughout the nineteenth and early twentieth centuries, New Orleanians did their grocery shopping at open-air markets run by the city. Built in 1875, the St. Roch Market was one of these city markets, and it supplied the neighborhood with groceries until the mid-1940s, when the city sold it to private owners. It was a small seafood market and po' boy shop until 2005, when it flooded during Katrina. The building sat vacant until 2015, when a huge renovation transformed it into its current iteration. Huge windows let in an abundance of light, reflected by the clean, white-tiled interior. The soaring ceiling is usually filled with the cacophony of dozens of patrons shopping and eating. The place is stunning, especially when you know how dilapidated it had become, but despite the makeover, its opening rankled some locals who were angry that the promised "market" was no more than a food hall.

What it is, though, is a restaurant incubator, and each of the stalls inside houses a rental space for purveyors of all sorts of cuisine, from baked goods to plate lunches. The one unchanging location in the market is the bar, Mayhaw. Named for a favorite local berry (try mayhaw jelly if you can), the bar offers a well-priced selection of wine and beer, as well as signature cocktails and seasonal favorites. You can even pick up some food from one of the stalls and carry it to the bar, or grab a drink from the bar and go sit at one of the food counters. The tile does not help with the crowd noise, and visiting can be challenging, but it's hard to resist hanging out in the market's lively atmosphere. When I want to talk without hollering, I take a seat in the back patio, away from traffic-heavy St. Claude. Despite the grumblings about gentrification, I'm glad the building has been so beautifully restored and has become a spot for nearby communities to eat and drink.

MIMI'S IN THE MARIGNY

2601 Royal St. • (504) 872-9868
HOURS 3 p.m.–4 a.m. Sun–Thur; 3 p.m.–5 a.m. Sat and Sun
NO HAPPY HOUR

Mimi's in the Marigny

Located at the corner of Franklin and Royal, Mimi's is a local hub of Marigny drinking. The downstairs bar is one spacious room, the abundance of wood making the space both warm and welcoming. High-top tables and stools placed adjacent to open windows allow patrons perched on them to enjoy the summer breeze, and the sounds of the street mingle with their conversations. For a good while, Mimi's was the only place in the neighborhood for those who wanted something more refined than a whiskey and soda or a Bud. I ordered my first Chimay here in the mid-1990s and was surprised when it was served in a specially branded glass. Although there are now other bars nearby with better beer lists, the wine selection remains reliable, with a solid glass of Spanish red still a remarkable $5. If that doesn't say neighborhood bar, nothing else will. I met some tourists who had been to Mimi's and loved it, though they kept calling it a dive bar. Dive bars don't have goat cheese on the menu or bartenders who can articulate the difference between a glass of Borsao and Rioja.

It takes a lot of folks to make the downstairs feel crowded. The high ceilings keep the room open, even when the room fills up and people have to sip their drinks around the pool table, dodging cues as players call shots. Upstairs is usually more tranquil, with low tables and sofas for cozy conversation. If you need to smoke or take a breather, step outside on a balcony, a rare rooftop view of the Marigny.

R BAR

1431 Royal St. • (504) 948-7499
www.royalstreetinn.com
HOURS 2 p.m.–til 7 days a week
NO HAPPY HOUR

When I first moved to New Orleans in 2001, I was not earning much money, so my drinking depended a lot on where I could do so cheaply. I soon became a fan of the R Bar, specifically what they called "The Special": a High Life and a shot of Jameson, a combination the rest of the world calls a "Boilermaker." Though my fortunes have improved, I am still a fan of that combo and find it astonishing that the price has only increased by a dollar. The R Bar still serves well-priced, well-poured drinks in a setting that was hipster before we knew that word.

The bar is dim even in the day, with tinted windows, dark walls, and red lighting. Even the baize on the pool table is red. The decor is eclectic. Behind the bar are portraits of three fans of New Orleans: Mark Twain, Napoleon, and Fats Domino, though the third "portrait" is really a close-up of his hand on piano keys, his diamond piano ring perched jauntily on his pinky. A papier-mâché pink bunny head completes the installation. If you are a fan of Dario Argento films or sci-fi b-movies, you'll enjoy the nightly selection of movies on view above the bar. If your wallet is thin but your hair is long, make sure to come on a Monday when you can get a haircut and shot for $10.

As crowded as this place can get with tourists peeling off Frenchmen, it still feels neighborhoody, and there is a kind of low-key vibe that is missing from the blare of Frenchmen and the bawdiness of Bourbon Street. I came here a few months ago and a cat jumped on the pool table, placing his paw inside one of the 6 holes. After it became clear that he wasn't moving, the game continued and everyone just played around him. Everyone just kept doing what they wanted, and everyone was happy—something Twain, Napoleon and Fats can all probably agree on.

THREE MUSES

536 Frenchmen St. • (504) 252-4801
www.3musesnola.com
HOURS 5 p.m.–10 p.m. Wed–Sun; 5 p.m.–11 p.m. Fri and Sat
NO HAPPY HOUR

This spot is really a music venue, I know, but it also offers some of the most delicious and interesting cocktails that you can get on Frenchmen, a street more focused on high-caliber tunes than drinks. On my last visit here, I went with my friend Mark, a transplant from New York who has lived in New Orleans on and off for the last ten years. We went for one drink and stayed for three. He noted that everything he loves about New Orleans is here in Three Muses: good food, good drinks and good music. When you step back and critically assess the space, you realize it's a pretty bare room, though it doesn't feel that way at all. Instead, it feels, well, beautiful. Lovely black and white photographs of musicians adorn the walls, attesting to the club's musical focus. I asked Mark to imagine what the room would feel like if a band wasn't playing here, and he aptly observed that you can't remove them. The jazz musicians are an integral part of tonight's scene, framed as they are by a large picture window against the street. I wish that the area dedicated to drinking, the bar itself, were bigger, so that more drinkers could enjoy the gorgeous drinks produced under the eagle eye of Kimberly Patton Bragg. I have followed "KPB" from bar to bar across the city, and I remain constantly impressed by her creativity and talent. The Champagne Supernova was a tingly, bubbly standout; Mark had three, and after I sampled the Here Without Me (also good but better for winter), I joined him. The grapefruit/champagne/Lillet concoction was refreshing after tromping down Frenchmen in the heat. When you go to Three Muses, the bar will probably be crowded. Be persistent. Order your drink and hang out until one of the seats becomes available. Or better yet, go early and plant yourself at the bar to enjoy New Orleans's holy trinity of music, drinks, and beauty.

YUKI IZAKAYA

525 Frenchmen St. • (504) 943-1122
No website
HOURS 6:30 p.m.–midnight 7 days a week
NO HAPPY HOUR

This diminutive, narrow setting is a far cry from the rest of Frenchmen Street. Japanese travel and movie posters adorn the walls, and the bar is crowned with a clowder of golden lucky cats greeting patrons as they enter. Anime films (with subtitles) light up one wall, and flags depicting the rising sun cover the other. It seems like there is no room for musicians in the petite space, but they find a way somehow. You can hear live music here most nights. Unlike the brass bands whose thundering din dominates the rest of Frenchmen Street, the music at Yuki is chill, often smooth Brazilian or quiet jazz.

In Japan, Izakaya are traditional Japanese gastropubs, where patrons gather to enjoy sake and bar snacks. Yuki serves a formidable list of sakes that include dry, floral, hot, cold, and milky unfiltered versions. Or you can sample shochu, a Japanese liquor distilled from sugar cane, sweet potato, barley, tea, rice or other bases. The kitchen serves until late, and though there is no sushi, the fried chicken is apparently a favorite among musicians who work gigs on the street.

Big in Japan at Yuki

CHAPTER 3

Tremé

T remé (pronounced TRUH-MAY) is the oldest black neighborhood in America, and many argue it is the birthplace of jazz. Often still referred to by its French name, Faubourg Tremé, it was named for Claude Tremé, a real estate developer who settled in New Orleans in 1783 and owned a small part of the neighborhood. In the eighteenth and nineteenth centuries, both free persons of color as well as African slaves who had obtained their freedom owned property in this neighborhood. This remarkable achievement, when the country was so immersed in slavery, was facilitated by flexible French and Spanish laws concerning property ownership, as well as the presence of a large population of free people of color as compared to other large southern cities. The heart of Tremé was Congo Square, a gathering place for both slaves and free people of color in that time. It now lies inside Armstrong Park, named for New Orleans's native son Louis Armstrong. St. Augustine Church, the oldest African-American Catholic Church in the country, is located here, as is St. Louis Cemetery #1, the final resting place of civil rights activist Homer Plessy and New Orleans's most famous Voodoo Queen, Marie Laveau.

BULLET'S SPORTS BAR
2441 A P Tureaud Ave. • (504) 669-4464
No website
HOURS 8 a.m.–midnight (or later if a band is playing) 7 days a week

The crowd at Bullet's all know each other, and if you stick around long enough, by the end of the night they will know you, too. Bullet's neighborhood vibe is best experienced on Sunday nights, when a rotating selection of musicians serenade the crowd. Come a little early, between five and six in the evening, and you will find rows of tables lined up, each marked with a sign reading "Reserved." One table is for "Flint," another is for "Ms Pat." Slowly but surely, the regulars arrive at their tables, which are already prepared with their "set-ups" (a bucket of ice and glasses). Each table then sends an emissary to the bar to buy a half-pint (or more) of their favorite spirit. Soon the room fills, as do the tables, and it's apparent that this arrangement allows one to host friends to drinks but it also keeps the bar from getting too crowded with folks waiting to order one drink at a time. The good news is that it's free to reserve a table; you only need to call ahead and then make sure to arrive before the music starts (otherwise they give away your spot).

Other nights, the tables are moved away to make room for dancing, whether to R&B or zydeco on the jukebox, or to the raucous beat of the Pinettes, an all-female brass band. Bullet's is not handy for most tourists, but if you want a taste of a truly local night out in New Orleans, get yourself there.

KERMIT'S TREMÉ MOTHER-IN-LAW LOUNGE

1500 N. Claiborne Ave. • (504) 975-3955
www.facebook.com/Kermits-Treme-Motherinlaw-Lounge
HOURS 5 p.m.–midnight (or later) 7 days a week
NO HAPPY HOUR

When you first arrive at the Mother-in-Law, you'll notice some rather remarkable murals covering the building. One depicts a woman and man who appear to be ascending to heaven. Others contain unusual phrases: "I'm a Charity Hospital Baby" and "Emperor of the Universe." These are portraits and testaments to the bar's original owners: Ernie and Antoinette K-Doe, and to understand what the bar means to residents as well as to the larger New Orleans music scene, you first need to know about this couple.

Ernie K-Doe was a rhythm and blues singer in New Orleans, famous for his song "Mother-in-Law," which reached #1 on the charts in 1961. Though K-Doe never had another national hit, he remained a popular musician who

Ernie K-Doe and Miss Antoinette memorialized on the side of the Mother-in-Law Lounge

became even more famous in town because of his outlandish and bombastic personality. He often referred to himself as "The Emperor of the Universe," and he took to wearing a cape and crown. In 1994, he and his wife, Antoinette, opened The Mother-in-Law Lounge, and it became a hub for performing musicians of all stripes.

The Mother-in-Law Lounge is located on Claiborne Avenue. It was once a beautiful thoroughfare in this historically black neighborhood, a tree-lined gathering place where neighbors could stroll and visit. When the interstate was built in the 1970s, Claiborne no longer served as a community hub. The Mother-in-Law's presence along Claiborne recreated (on a smaller scale) a place for neighbors to meet. Often crowds from the bar will spill out, not only into the parking lot but also across the street, under the interstate overpass.

When Ernie died in 2001, Miss Antoinette (as locals called her) continued to run the place. She also commissioned a mannequin of her husband, dressed in his elaborate costumes and capes, that was usually propped up at the club. Occasionally, Miss Antoinette would take the statue out with her to other places, and you would see photos of the two of them eating dinner or at another club.

The Mother-in-Law Lounge was severely damaged during Katrina, but it was rebuilt and reopened in 2006 through the efforts of volunteers. Miss Antoinette kept those volunteers fed, serving pots of gumbo and beans that she cooked in the side yard of the bar. It was during this time, during a particularly divisive mayoral election, that Antoinette submitted K-Doe's name as a possible mayoral candidate, despite him being deceased for more than five years. Though her actions were tongue in cheek, the idea took off, and "K-Doe for Mayor" T-shirts and bumper stickers appeared around town. These sales helped Miss Antoinette rebuild the bar. In 2006, artist Daniel Fuselier started painting murals on the building as part of the rebuilding

Tipplers taking a smoke break outdoors at Sidney's Saloon

efforts. He continues to add to the murals, reflecting changes in the bar and New Orleans music scene.

Miss Antoinette died in 2009 on Mardi Gras day after suffering a heart attack. Just a few days before, she and K-Doe's mannequin had ridden on a float as grand marshals in the Krewe of Muses's Mardi Gras parade.

After her death, the Mother-in-Law was shuttered for some time, until local trumpeter Kermit Ruffins took it over and reopened the bar in 2014. Its reopening was greeted with much appreciation and even relief. Some worried the club would be bought and the name might be changed, but Ruffins made sure to keep Mother-in-Law in the name. Musicians and DJs once again appear most evenings.

One of the main murals on the building shows the K-Does in full celestial splendor. But the bar is not merely a shrine to the K-Does; every performance there keeps the original spirit of the K-Does going. As K-Doe used to say, "You just good, that's all!"

SIDNEY'S SALOON

1200 St. Bernard Ave. • (504) 224-2672
HOURS 3 p.m.–3 a.m. every day
HAPPY HOUR 3 p.m.–7 p.m.
$5 beer and a shot, $2.50 domestic beer, $4.50 drafts, $3 well drinks

Sidney's is named for its original owner, a musician who ran the place in the 1950s. On my most recent visit, a patron sitting next to me remembered coming to Sidney's when Sidney himself still ran the bar. When I told him he didn't look old enough to have been in a bar in the 1950s, he laughed and said it was when he was ten years old, but back then it was OK for children to come by a bar and get a cold drink or even pick up a beer for their parents. In the 1960s, laws changed, prohibiting youngsters from hanging out in such establishments. He chuckled, "I could come here when I was ten but not when I was fifteen!"

It's not unusual to sit next to a regular like that at Sidney's. Though the place has changed hands a few times in recent years, it seems the clientele has remained the same, and everybody knows each other. During a different visit, a man who lives around the corner, Roberto, brought in a big bowl of homemade ceviche, made from fish he had caught that morning. He placed the bowl along with a bag of tortilla chips on a table near the bar, and all the patrons sampled his recipe. Soon, patrons were buying rounds of Tecate beer to wash down his spicy gift.

Despite its age, Sidney's has kept up with the times. Their beer list has expanded under its newest owner, and the number of regional craft beers exceeds the standard big brands. Sidney's also has two daiquiri machines that churn out slushy cocktails. My favorite is The Perfect Storm, their version of a Dark and Stormy. Though fairly close to Frenchmen Street, Sidney's is worlds away from that touristy spot. It's full of locals and full of charm.

CHAPTER 4

Mid-City

Mid-City played an important role in the city's creation. One of its most defining features is Bayou St. John, and today you can find folks paddling kayaks down its shallow waters or strolling along its banks with cocktails in hand. But back in the eighteenth century, it was an important waterway for Native Americans who used it to access other aquatic arteries throughout the southern part of what is now Louisiana. Though the Bayou did not adjoin the Mississippi River, it was near enough that natives could pick up their canoes and carry them to the river to trade on a larger scale. This path, called a portage in French, was shown to the French explorers who saw the possibilities it created and decided to build their new city at the junction of the road and the Mississippi River. This pathway, now called Bayou Road, connects with Esplanade Avenue and ultimately the French Quarter. It's why the first Louisiana governor's house, the Pitot House, was built along the bayou. Now seemingly far from the action of the city, back then this house lay in the thick of trade. The other dominant feature of Mid-City is City Park, laid out by Frederick Law Olmsted, the man responsible for New York's Central Park. Its 1,300-plus verdant acres merit a trip and offer a natural green escape from bustling downtown.

Mid-City's vibe today reflects its slight distance from downtown, and many of its restaurants and bars are low-key, relaxed neighborhood establishments that cater to a local clientele.

BAYOU BEER GARDEN

326 N. Jefferson Davis Pkwy. • (504) 302-9357
www.bayoubeergarden.com
HOURS 11 a.m.–2 a.m. 7 days a week
NO HAPPY HOUR

BAYOU WINE GARDEN

315 N Rendon St. • (504) 826-2925
www.bayouwinegarden.com
HOURS 11 a.m.–2 a.m. 7 days a week
NO HAPPY HOUR

Located on opposite sides of the same block, the Bayou Beer Garden and Bayou Wine Garden are technically two different bars. However, a wonderful courtyard connects them, and between the two they offer something for every kind of drinker. From the Jefferson Davis side of the block, you will find the Bayou Beer Garden. The bar boasts a robust selection of local, regional and national craft brews on a rotating list of taps. While the inside is a convivial space, don't neglect the outside. If it's sunny, grab a chair in

Just a portion of the large outdoor seating at Bayou Beer and Wine Gardens

the shade on the covered section of the massive deck. Or, in cooler weather, move to the exterior section of the deck and soak up some Vitamin D with your brew. The beer garden's many tables accommodate large groups, but the patio itself is so big that even when it's crowded, you never feel like you're joining someone else's party.

Beer not your thing? No worry, just keep walking through the back of the beer garden into the newly added wine garden, where you can choose a glass from over 150 wines, many on tap. The patio wine bar usually has twelve wines on tap with more available inside the wine bar. While the beer garden mostly serves pub-style fare, the wine bar serves more posh items like meats cured in-house and cheese plates. This end of the patio is also a little more upscale. Expansive awnings shade patrons, and a handsome brick fountain offers additional seating while serving as a decorative water feature. If rain comes, as it often does in New Orleans, you can escape to the lovely wine bar adjacent to the patio.

There's the old saying that you can't be everything to everyone, but I gotta tell ya, the Bayou Beer/Wine Garden empire comes close. You can happily drink inside or out. You can bring your dog. If you plan your drinking accordingly, it's not expensive. It's the kind of place where you go for a round and before you know it, day has turned to night.

FINN MCCOOL'S

3701 Banks St. • (504) 486-9080
www.finnmccools.com
HOURS 8 a.m. (or earlier if there is soccer on)–2 a.m. or 3 a.m.
NO HAPPY HOUR

Finn McCool's is both the epitome of a neighborhood bar and a haven for fans of foreign sports. At all hours of the day, you'll find not only international broadcasts of soccer, rugby, and cricket, but also ardent fans decked out in their team colors, exchanging dueling songs with their opponents. It often starts early and continues throughout the day, as the crowds of fans enter and leave, almost in shifts—like factory work, but oh so much better. From the British Premier League to the Bundesliga, from Liga MX to MLS, from British to Aussie Rugby, they show it all.

Bartenders serve a perfectly poured Guinness at Finn McCool's

But Finn's (as locals often call it) is so much more than a sports bar. It is a community bar, one that hosts programming that encourages neighbors to meet one another. Sure there's trivia, but there's also an occasional Field Day, with three-legged and wheelbarrow races, just like you played in middle school. The kickball league in New Orleans, now twenty teams strong, started at Finn's. If you bring them your turkey the week of Thanksgiving, they will fry it for you. They even host potlucks for Saints games: Finn's provides the meat, patrons bring the sides, and the resulting meal is free to anyone in the bar.

This belief that a bar is more than just a place to drink comes straight from its founders, Pauline and Stephen Patterson, who came to New Orleans from Ireland and tried to recreate the sensibility of an Irish pub. They succeeded. In 2015, the *Irish Times* named it one of the ten best Irish pubs outside of Ireland. We didn't necessarily need that confirmation from the motherland, but it's nice to have it all the same.

PAL'S LOUNGE

949 N. Rendon St. • (504) 488-7257

No website

HOURS 3 p.m.–3 a.m. Mon–Thu; 3 p.m.–4 a.m. Fri and Sat

HAPPY HOUR 3 p.m.–7 p.m. Mon–Sat

When I agreed to tackle the task of writing a guide to the bars of New Orleans, I set two rules. Rule #1: I would visit or revisit every bar I wrote about, and would not write any entries based on my memories of the bar. Rule #2: I did not have to drink at every bar I visited. Drinking on deadline is a different experience than drinking while out with friends. You have to stay sober-ish, pay attention, and take legible notes to do justice to each spot. And I pretty much stuck to these rules. Well, at least the first one.

The night I revisited Pal's, I had decided that it was one of the bars that I was not going to drink at. I usually saved my drinking for places that specialized in cocktails, choosing club soda or a Coke at neighborhood joints when I needed a break from booze. Then I walked into Pal's. It's really hard to not drink in a bar you love, and I sure do love Pal's. It truly is one of those great neighborhood spots where the bartender treats you like an old friend. We walked in and were greeted by Trent. When we said we needed a minute to decide what to drink, he affably replied, "Take your time. You've got till 3 a.m." It's a bar that feels lived in, like a den or your parents' basement. Your mom would probably not have displayed the 1960s-era portraits of naked ladies, however tasteful they may be, but she certainly would have allowed the air hockey table. The cushy black bar stools with their brass rivets give the bar a sense of class, and for all the use they have seen, they're in remarkably good shape. Pal's is worn but not dilapidated. When I visited, the bar's lone TV showed Francois Truffaut's *400 Blows*, but it gets tuned to Saints games when football season arrives.

After a visit to the ladies' room, I checked in with Trent about the sole piece of graffiti that adorns the wall. It says "Laura Izzo, please come home." I asked him if that was the same Laura who used to work at the Shim Sham, which is now One Eyed Jacks. He said it was and that he used to work with her there. Pal's is owned by the same people who owned the Shim Sham, so they shared a lot of staff. Laura moved away from New Orleans to go to graduate school in 2004 and I haven't thought about her much since then.

Drinking by City Park at Ralph's on the Park

But when she left, someone wrote that plea on the wall at Pal's, and since then, whenever Trent repaints the bathroom, he paints around that sentence.

New Orleans bars are full of these interconnections and moments marking someone's arrival to or departure from the city. This is a city where bars encourage a special kind of memory making, and Pal's in particular is a great place to make a new one or be reminded of an old one.

RALPH'S ON THE PARK

900 City Park Ave. • (504) 488-1000
www.ralphsonthepark.com
HOURS 5:30–9 p.m. Sun–Thur, 5:30–9:30 p.m. Fri–Sat,
Lunch daily 11:30 a.m.–2 p.m. except Sat and Mon
HAPPY HOUR 3 p.m.–6 p.m. 7 days a week

In 2003, restaurateur Ralph Brennan took over the building where Ralph's on the Park resides now. He held a meeting for members of the community to come and learn about the new project. You would think the first question neighbors asked Ralph would be about parking or noise management, all valid concerns for those living near a new restaurant. Instead, the first question was "Can we drink at the bar?" Apparently the previous owner of the locale didn't allow anyone to come sit at the bar and just have a drink. Instead, he limited bar access to those who were waiting to dine. When Ralph learned of this, it cemented his plan to reorganize the bar space. In the old restaurant, the bar was an afterthought, stuck in the back of the dining room. Now the bar occupies its own welcoming spot where locals can come for an after-work nip or an evening nightcap.

The previous restaurant's windows were curtained off, but the windows at Ralph's bar are open, allowing drinkers an unimpeded view of the ancient oaks that grace the park. Ralph wanted to bring the park into the space, and indeed, sitting in the bar feels like sitting on the back porch of the best backyard in town. Even the decor reminds patrons of the location. The walls are papered with images of New Orleanians enjoying the park that were pulled directly from the City Park Archives. My favorite posting is in the ladies' room and features a beauty contestant who won not just a trophy, but a turkey as well! The drinks menu at Ralph's sticks with competently poured classics that appeal to Mid-City neighbors. Ralph's on the Park is a worthy spot if you are visiting the New Orleans Museum of Art or City Park. Pop in and drink like a local.

REVEL

133 N. Carrollton Ave. • (504) 309-6122
revelcafeandbar.com
HOURS 11 a.m.–11 p.m. 7 days a week
HAPPY HOUR 11 a.m.–7 p.m. 7 days a week

Chris McMillan is one of the most respected bartenders in New Orleans, and fans of his well-crafted drinks and equally inventive stories have followed him all around town. After manning the cocktail programs at the Ritz and Kingfish, he and his wife, Laura, have finally opened their own spot on Carrolton, just a block off the streetcar line. I only wish the bar was longer so that it could accommodate everyone who wants to chat with Chris.

Tuesday summer nights are normally a bit quiet in New Orleans, but not here. Each seat at the bar is packed with cocktail aficionados sipping on Chris's libations. The menu requires some time to read, with each page dedicated to a different era in the growth of the cocktail. At the bar, brass elephants wrap their trunks around a brass arm rail and raise it aloft. Laura tells us that the bar came from Kentucky and at one point in its history was the bar for a strip club. We can see cigarette burns along its top, marks of its own history. Chris even had additional elephants made to match the originals on the bar to extend the rail. When we look closely we can see that the newer ones are shinier and lack the patina of the older ones. Lee observes the only way to age them is having people rub them, lean on them and spill their drinks on them. We wonder what those elephants have seen, and what they will never forget. Patrons lean in and listen to Chris's stories. We join them, doing our part to help the new elephants catch up with the old.

TREO

3835 Tulane Ave. • (504) 304-4878
www.treonola.com
HOURS 4 p.m.–midnight 7 days a week
HAPPY HOUR 4 p.m.–7 p.m.

When you walk into Treo, look up and take in the extraordinary map of New Orleans, constructed from reclaimed wood. A faded green door stands in for City Park, and a cream-colored, domed light fixture is the perfect replica of the Superdome. There's another map of the city and its environs on the wall, and patrons are invited to stick pins into it to mark their homes. The Mid-City section looks like a pincushion, but there's still plenty of room as you stretch out. Unlike its sister bar, Finn McCool's over on Banks Street, whose focus is whiskey and beer, Treo serves some great cocktails.

Treo is brought to us by the good folks at Finn McCool's, who know a thing or two about creating a warm, neighborhood vibe. The cocktails are imaginative and seasonal. The summer menu features The Mistress, their

Treo and its beautiful city map that watches over its patrons

riff on the French 75, featuring gin, blueberry syrup and sparkling rosé; the spicy Sunda Selat showcases a house-infused cumin and jalapeño bourbon mixed with lime. Patrons who like something more traditional can choose from a whole page of standards including the Old Fashioned, Blood and Sand, and the Vieux Carré, each offered for the bargain price of $7. Indeed, this part of the menu feels a bit like a challenge, and Lee and I have steadily worked to complete the list.

The amiable environment is augmented by a friendly and knowledge-able staff that is happy to answer questions about unfamiliar ingredients. On a slow night, bar manager Tyler Chauvin may even share her enthusiasm for (and a small sample of) their collection of unfamiliar vermouths and amaros. Treo also features an art gallery and frequently has openings featuring local artists' work. If the gallery is open, it's certainly worth a visit. The owners, Pauline and Stephen Patterson, really love this section of Mid-City and have worked hard to support its revitalization. Treo is their gift to their neighbors: a friendly date-night spot with great drinks in a beautifully renovated space.

TWELVE MILE LIMIT

500 S. Telemachus St. • (504) 488-8114
www.facebook.com/twelve.mile.limit
HOURS 5 p.m.–2 a.m. Mon–Fri; 10 a.m.–2 a.m. Sat; 10 a.m.–midnight Sun
HAPPY HOUR 5 p.m.–7 p.m. and, on weeknights, another happy hour after midnight

During Prohibition, ships that wanted to serve their passengers alcohol had to wait until they were twelve miles away from American shores before they could break out the booze. Some ships never got any further, dropping anchor a few feet past the limit and turning into floating bars, thumbing their noses at impotent Coast Guard vessels that couldn't make an arrest since the crew was not, technically, breaking the law. This kind of cheeky, even gleeful, attitude toward drinking defines the vibe at Twelve Mile Limit.

When T. Cole Newton opened Twelve Mile Limit back in 2010, his goal was to create a neighborhood cocktail bar, a new concept in New Orleans. Back then, if you wanted a well-made cocktail, you had to go to a high-end establishment and be prepared to pay a high rent for that fancy drink and fancy chair. If you went to your local watering hole, you ordered whiskey and soda, paid cash, and liked it. Newton was savvy enough to see where the wind was blowing in the cocktail world, and he took his experience making drinks at Commander's Palace and brought it to slightly divier environs. The casual atmosphere and funky decor belie the thoughtful, well-made libations. $7 craft cocktails in your neighborhood bar? Can't afford not to.

Favorite drinks include the namesake Twelve Mile Limit, a mixture of rum, brandy, rye, lime and pomegranate syrup; and The Baudin (the name of the bar's cross street), a spicy concoction of whiskey, honey and cayenne. A small but curated bottle and draft list keep beer fans happy. The kitchen serves good BBQ, a great base for boozing, and the patio in back offers a bit of quiet when the bar gets crowded and noisy. Twelve Mile's calendar is full of trivia nights, comedy nights, live dating games, and a regularly occurring Heatwave Dance Party, but my favorite nights at the bar involve chatting with friends or the bartender about local city gossip. It's nice to have the option of a place like Twelve Mile Limit, where you can drink a perfectly made Old Fashioned in a tank top and shorts while watching a live dating show called The Hump Connection.

Pauline and Stephen Patterson

When I asked Pauline and Stephen Patterson what brought them to New Orleans, Stephen laughed and said "Oh, it's a cliché. We got off the boat (OK, the plane) with $100 in our pocket." Pauline corrected him, saying "No, actually he had $175 and I had $200." In college, the two had fallen in love with the city on a vacation in 1988. When they graduated in 1990, they crossed the pond to start a life in New Orleans.

Both worked as bartenders in Irish pubs in the city, and both were told by patrons that they should open their own place. So, in 2002, while Pauline was working as a real estate agent, the two bought a rundown building on Banks Street in Mid-City that even her clients didn't want. After a significant renovation, they opened Finn McCool's, or "Finn's" if you're a local.

The Pattersons' vision of Finn's was always informed by how pubs function in Ireland. They are not merely places to get a beer; they are community centers. As Stephen puts it, "If you need a job, you come to Finn's; if you need your roof fixed, you come to Finn's; if

you need someone to watch your dog while you are away, you come to Finn's." Neighbors responded to this ethos, and soon Finn's became a hub for this section of Mid-City.

Then Katrina destroyed the bar. For a time, the Pattersons considered leaving. Their insurance company, like many others at the time, refused to honor their policies. They had no source of income. But soon residents came by with offers of help, and Finn's became a shining beacon of possibility in a sea of darkness and desolation. The Pattersons threw five parties over the course of the renovation, marking moments of progress. The first party happened when they'd completed the demolition and the place was gutted, and the last occurred when the electricity was finally turned on. They did not charge anyone to come to any of these celebrations. Stephen remembers that at the last party, there were more people behind the bar than in front of it. "Everyone felt a part of the place." Some had washed the building, some had fixed a door, some had painted. "They told us they would not have been back in New Orleans if it hadn't been for us. But we wouldn't have been back if it wasn't for them."

It is this acknowledgement of the interconnectedness of the Pattersons and their work with the neighborhood and the city that led them to open their second spot, Treo. "Everyone always told us we should open a bar Uptown, but we didn't want to dilute Finn's." Pauline noted that Mid-City needed another "date night" place, so in 2012, they bought a dilapidated bar on Tulane Avenue and turned it into a charming spot that also functions as a gallery for local artists' work. Pauline went to art college and, when possible, tries to add to the beauty of the city, in particular Mid-City. This led her to work with the City Council to expand the Museum and City Park Cultural Products District to include Tulane Avenue. Buildings in this area are able to sell art at discounted tax rates as well as receive tax credits when they renovate structures within its boundaries. Pauline worked to create this designation so that other folks would be incentivized to help improve the avenue despite the fact that she and Stephen had already finished Treo and would not receive the benefits.

"I learned a long time ago that I can't fix everything that is wrong here. I can only do my part and encourage other people to do their part." That sensibility defines the Pattersons and their properties. Whether the bars are hosting artists' work, fundraising for charity, or merely introducing two neighbors to each other, they want to make the city they love as good as it can be. As Stephen notes, "We want people to get more out of Finn's than we get out of them." How nice when all of that can happen over a pint.

CHAPTER 5

Central Business District and Warehouse District

Standing among the multi-story hotels, condos, and office buildings of the Central Business District, it's easy to forget that this part of town was once as residential as the French Quarter. Unfortunately, most of the houses built then were torn down in the early twentieth century to create hotels, high rises and city government buildings. Further upriver is the Warehouse District, named for the many warehouses that stored cotton, sugar, and coffee back when port activity still happened near here. This section is also home to many buildings that once served as "exchanges" where these commodities were traded. Now they, too, are condos, full of people instead of cotton. The bars here really serve the people who work here. If you are looking for places with happening happy hours, this is ground zero.

ACE LOUNGE/ALTO POOL BAR
600 Carondelet St. • (504) 900-1180
www.acehotel.com/neworleans
HOURS Lobby bar 11 a.m.–2 a.m.; Alto pool bar 10 a.m.–9 p.m.
HAPPY HOUR 3 p.m.–6 p.m. 7 days a week

The Ace hotel opened in 2015 and is already the cool kid hangout in the Central Business District. Despite my propensity to roll my eyes at the newest, latest thing, I have to admit, the lounge has won me over. It feels like the living room (a very large living room) of a world traveller, decorated with art and decor collected along the way. African drums double as low tables. Plush rugs and groupings of furniture scattered across the terrazzo floor create conversational islands, which add intimacy to the cavernous room. The acoustics are not conducive to romance (it's noisy in here) but they do help make the space feel lively, even when there aren't many people in it. The drinks are top notch; the Ace poached some quality bartenders from around town to work here, and both their original and classic drinks are spot on.

Drinks are equally solid at the rooftop pool bar, Alto. For a hotel pool, it sure draws a lot of locals, and according to several friends, it is the new place for millennials to meet both for work meetings and after work. Sounds good to me. Financial forecasts are always best discussed over a cocktail with your toes in the water. One sunny spring day, there were about fifty people at Alto, and I knew four of them. Everyone had a drink. The music was lively. Though summer was several months away, it felt like we were all on vacation. One friend has noted that while the space is trendy, it doesn't feel very familiar. Or, as he put it, "It feels like what someone in L.A. thinks New Orleans looks like." He might have a point. The quirky-but-still-beautiful staff, in their slightly disheveled, mismatched outfits, seem too curated to be real. Pair them with a bevy of well-groomed, thin, young people cavorting around a pool, and the whole scene feels very California. Not that this is a bad thing, just not something you see often in New Orleans.

The pool bar isn't as robust as that downstairs, but the staff here are as well trained as their colleagues. I ordered an Aviation off the menu and my bartender made it without blinking. I'll be going back, for sure. No point in avoiding hanging out at a gorgeous pool for the price of a drink (a reasonable $6 at that) just because my wardrobe isn't from H&M and I crossed forty several birthdays ago. Not with summer approaching, the prospect of an Aviation in a plastic cup, and a view few places can beat.

CAPDEVILLE

520 Capdeville St. • (504) 371-5161

www.capdevillenola.com

HOURS 11 p.m.–2:30 p.m. and 5 p.m.–11 p.m. Mon–Thur; 11 p.m.–midnight Fri; 10:30 a.m.–midnight Sat; open for all Saints games on Sundays

HAPPY HOUR 4:30 p.m.–7 p.m. Mon–Thu; 11 a.m.–7 p.m. Friday

The first time I went to Capdeville, I got lost. It took me fifteen minutes of circling streets before I finally pulled out my phone and found the bar's one-block-long namesake street. But once you know where to look, this hidden gem of a bar is worth a stop.

Capdeville is an angel investor's candy store. It's located at the base of the IP building, home of the hip co-working space Launch Pad. The Idea Village, a vibrant resource for New Orleans entrepreneurs, is also a tenant. Guess what kind of patron is drinking in the bar? Earnest souls with big ideas, chatting about the city's latest startup. In the evening, the crowd can thin out, leaving room for the rest of us to enjoy some well-made cocktails in a bar adorned with dozens of Rebel Yell whiskey bottles, my new favorite "decor." I'm also a fan of their mac and cheese, and the gastropub feel extends to the atmosphere, which is warm and cozy. Capdeville is also one of the city's best-kept secrets if you are downtown drinking during the wildly popular Wednesdays at the Square, a free concert series that runs during the fall and spring. The concerts are fun, but if you need to get away from the hullabaloo, you can sneak across Camp Street to Capdeville for a pour of whiskey or a well-made Old Fashioned.

CATAHOULA

914 Union St. • (504) 603-2442

www.catahoulahotel.com

HOURS Pisco bar 7 a.m.–11 p.m. 7 days a week

NO HAPPY HOUR

One of the happy perks of the craft cocktail movement is the ready availability of exotic liquors. Pisco, a brandy from Chile and Peru, is one of these new darlings of the spirit world, and it is the star of the bar in the Catahoula Hotel.

Catahoula features this brandy in a myriad of applications. The eponymous Pisco Sour mixes the spirit with lime, sugar, and an egg white, all of which are shaken to a frothy foam and garnished with a few drops of Angostura bitters. It's a lovely, light drink, and like many classics, it can easily go wrong if the bartender is not careful to balance the ingredients. My friend Hillary, who spent time in Chile, gave it her stamp of approval, and I concurred. But Pisco Sours are not the only pisco drinks on the menu. There's a delicious punch on offer, and fans of Negronis and other bitter drinks will enjoy the unusual pisco and tonic. This drink is "garnished" with a slowly melting Campari-flavored ice cube that infuses the drink with its bitter and tart notes.

Ice, supervised by "Ice Chef" Hope Clarke, is as much of a star at this bar as the drinks themselves. She oversees the creation of dozens of cubes and spheres, some of which are hand-chopped specifically for a particular drink. Ice Chef seems a precious idea until you start to think of it as an ingredient—water quality and surface area play a huge role in the taste, temperature and dilution of your drink. But Clarke doesn't merely oversee the clear ice used in the cocktails. She also fashions the many liquor popsicles, cotton candy, and gummies featured in the bar's over-the-top booze feast: the Drunk Tank. This platter of liquor feels like a nod to the celebratory, over-the-top spirit of tiki, not surprising since bar manager Nathan Dalton left Tiki Tolteca to open this spot.

You really feel the playfulness of both bartenders in the rooftop bar, which serves boozy, icy, slushy drinks inspired by New Orleans's love affair with frozen daiquiris but prepared with more attention to craft and taste. Though the roof has no pool, it offers a lovely view of downtown and is a quieter, more chill spot than the rooftop at the Ace just down the street. If you've never tried pisco, you can't go wrong with the classic sour. But for me, the Drunk Tank is the way to go. Go big or go home. Or, in this case, go big, then go home.

CELLAR DOOR

916 Lafayette St. • (504) 265-8392
www.cellardoornola.com
HOURS 4:30 p.m.–midnight Mon–Thu; 4 p.m.–2 a.m. Fri; 5 p.m.–2 a.m. Sat; Sun only open for Saints home games
NO HAPPY HOUR

The sign announcing Cellar Door doesn't point to a door but rather a narrow walkway. That unassuming entrance is only one element of what makes this little jewel box so appealing. Cellar Door is housed in one of the oldest buildings in the city on this side of Canal Street. Set on Lafayette, a street stretching only a few blocks with no parking, it was once the site of a bordello. An element of that coy, hidden charm remains. Step into the space. Head left to the small bar. Or, turn right and settle onto a settee under a massive chandelier dripping crystals lifted straight from Storyville. The old New Orleans brick contrasts with modern art, including pieces by Jamie Reid, whose work graced Sex Pistols albums. The juxtaposition of old and new defines the bar, including its drinks menu, which has separate lists of both classics and some newer inventions like A Day at the Races, which balanced the sweetness of a Mint Julep with crème de cassis and lemon. Their happy hour is robust and deep: good snacks and $6 classics like an Old Fashioned or Daiquiri. Cellar Door's owners feel that "it is possible to be progressive and forward thinking, without compromising the cultural integrity of one's historic surroundings." A great concept for a new kind of bar, in downtown's oldest building.

CIRCLE BAR

1032 St. Charles Ave. • (504) 588-2616
www.circlebarneworleans.com
HOURS 4 p.m. 7 days a week
HAPPY HOUR 4 p.m.–7 p.m. 7 days a week

The Circle Bar was one of my haunts for a while. It was once the home of Elizabeth Cohen, the first woman doctor in Louisiana, back in the late nineteenth century. I enjoyed drinking in what had been an examining room. Its ceiling was adorned with a huge clock acquired from the headquarters of the now defunct K&B drugstore chain. We used to joke that when you danced under that clock, the concept of time lost all meaning. You could emerge from the Circle Bar and either discover you had only been there an hour or that it was now the next day.

Circle Bar occupies a powerful place in my memory because of a special night I spent there right after Hurricane Katrina. This book doesn't focus on what locals call The Storm much, except in the context of a bar closing or reopening due to its impact. In many ways the city has moved on, and I don't want visitors to feel it is all we think about. But for those of us who lived here and came back, it was a transformative experience. And many of the moments that kept us sane amid the craziness happened in bars.

I evacuated for two months after Katrina. Once I returned in early November, the city was just beginning to fill, and not a lot was open, but whenever possible I tried to meet up with friends I had not seen in months. One spot where we often went was the Circle Bar. One night in particular stands out. I went to hear a band, Egg Yolk Jubilee. This band is huge, eight or nine players, plenty of horns. The Circle Bar is fairly tiny. There was barely enough room for the band and the audience. At one point they launched into a rendition of "St. James Infirmary," a song that got a lot of play during that time. The listeners and the musicians, we were all mingled together, surrounded by this sound. It was a joyous and terrible cacophony of hope and despair.

Every time I go there now, consciously or not, I think about those evenings and that difficult time in my city's history. And writing this book has merely cemented what I already knew. That bars may be places where we make memories, but they are also repositories of them. And how we think about a bar is defined not only by the decor or the drinks or the patrons or even the bartenders, but also by what happened there. The K&B clock is no longer on the ceiling. It broke and now rests in pieces on the wall of the men's room. But in my mind, it is still above us as we raise our hands and dance, as we raise our glasses and toast, with trepidation and hope.

COCKTAIL BAR AT WINDSOR COURT

300 Gravier St. • (504) 523- 6000
www.windsorcourthotel.com/cocktail-bar-windsor-court
HOURS 5 p.m.–til Thu–Sun
HAPPY HOUR 5 p.m.–7 p.m.

POLO CLUB

300 Gravier St,.
(504) 522-1992
http://www.windsorcourthotel.com/polo-club-lounge
HOURS 11:30 a.m.–midnight Mon–Thu; 11:30 a.m.–1 a.m. Fri and Sat;
11 a.m.–midnight Sun
NO HAPPY HOUR

Kent Westmoreland at the Windsor Court Cocktail Bar

Every time I enter the lobby of the Windsor Court, I think, "Man, this place smells so good." Then I see the tremendous floral arrangements placed around the room and think, "Wow, those flowers are gorgeous." Then I remember I came here to drink. The Windsor Court Hotel is elegant and formal, every facet tasteful, considered, and intentional, an equally apt description for the drinks they serve at the Cocktail Bar. The Cocktail Bar is headed by Kurt Westmorland, who was named 2015's Mixologist of the Year by *New Orleans* magazine and is singularly focused on creating the most perfect version of a cocktail that he can. His Vieux Carré is certainly a testament to that desire, as are his efforts to revive interest in some forgotten favorites such as the Queen's Cousin and the Corpse Reviver 2. As the head mixologist of the Windsor Court, he oversees the cocktail programs of both the Polo Club and the Cocktail Bar.

The Polo Club, on the second floor of the hotel, is a wonderful lounge, all dark wood and overstuffed chairs, best enjoyed while sipping old, expensive Scotch. Though they don't require jackets anymore, you might want to spruce up before grabbing a drink here, if only to match the surroundings. Anais St. John, a talented jazz chanteuse, performs there most weekends, and her silky, sultry voice is a perfect foil to the clubby English feel of the bar. It is a small, intimate, dim venue. In contrast, the Cocktail Bar, housed in the lobby, is open and spacious, and it doesn't take much to start seeing the whole space as your bar. When the Polo Club fills up, which it often does on weekends, it can be hard to find a seat and even harder to visit above the din. You'll have no such problems at the Cocktail Bar, where the entire lobby is at your disposal. Westmoreland has worked to transform the lobby bar from the Polo Club's "frumpy little sister" into a spot that is as welcoming to locals getting off work as it is for visitors seeking a nightcap. Even if you aren't a guest of the hotel, for a round or two, it feels like you are.

COMPÈRE LAPIN

535 Tchoupitoulas St. • (504) 599-2119
www.comperelapin.com
HOURS 11:30 p.m.–2:30 p.m./5:30–10 p.m. Mon–Fri; Sat til 11 p.m.;
Sun 3 p.m.–10 p.m.
HAPPY HOUR 3 p.m.–6 p.m. Mon–Fri

Abigail Gullo welcomes you to Compère Lapin

Compère Lapin is set in the Old 77 Hotel, which was once a coffee warehouse and later a chandlery (a.k.a. a general wholesale business), providing sailing ships with canvas, rope tobacco and other necessities. You can tell this was once a warehouse. The exposed beams and brick don't feel industrial, just historic. But the bar and lighting keep the feel modern. Depending on your point of view or expectations, you may either think of this as a classic New Orleans place or somewhere totally modern and hip. Regardless, this juxtaposition of styles means there is something here to make everyone feel at home.

The bar at Compère Lapin is under the direction of Abigail Gullo, who won the national title of Bartender of the Year in 2016. The bar is notable for its breadth and depth, and Gullo carries spirits that many bars in New Orleans do not. One example is Grand Poppy, a craft amaro from California that includes poppies in its recipe. She created a drink based around it, Wry Smile, which mixes the amaro with rhubarb, sherry, vermouth and rye. If you put yourself in her hands, you can really explore the bar's more unusual products.

Abigail is imaginative and her drinks are delicious, but I mostly go to drink at her bar because she is an amazingly generous and funny host. When I asked her about what it means to be a bartender, she explained that her focus when guests come into bar goes beyond making them feel welcome at her bar or her hotel. She is, instead, "welcoming them to the celebration that we throw every day in New Orleans." Locals know that something special happens in New Orleans every day, and it's her job to "help people in my bar navigate what kind of New Orleans day they are going to have."

HANDSOME WILLY'S

218 S. Robertson St. • (504) 525-0377
HOURS 11 a.m.–11 p.m. Mon–Thur; 11 a.m.–4 a.m. Fri; 5 p.m.–3 a.m. Sat
HAPPY HOUR 2 p.m.–6 p.m. Mon–Fri

I met my friend Erica at Handsome Willy's the other day, and when we arrived, we admitted to each other that we had each gotten lost en route. This is because neither of us had ever driven to Handsome Willy's. We had only gone when we were already stumbling out of a cab. I mention this because Handsome Willy's is not easy to get to by car. Though its hand-painted sign, which covers an entire exterior wall, acts as a beacon that can be seen from Interstate 10, once you start navigating the dead ends and one ways of downtown, you may wonder if you will ever get there. But persevere.

Handsome Willy's is the closest bar to the Tulane Avenue Medical Complex, which encompasses several hospitals and schools, and at 6 p.m. the bar was full of folks in scrubs, sipping an after-work beer. It was a strictly local crowd, and Handsome Willy's seems a mostly local bar. They even run tabs for privileged customers, including the man who acts as their delivery guy during lunch. Tonight he ordered a beer with promises to pay for it soon, and we watched Victoria (a truly charming bartender who has been behind the stick at Handsome Willy's since 2013) hang his tab on a small clothesline strung behind the bar. I'm sure this happens in other bars, but I can't tell you where. Also of note is the 10 percent discount offered for folks willing to pay by cash instead of by credit card.

The bar is chill and cozy, but we take our drinks to the patio, joining the other folks for some after-work winding down. Handsome Willy's has DJs most nights and crawfish boils on Saturdays when they are in season. The joint fills up on Sundays when the Saints play at home—the surrounding parking lots are filled with fans instead of medical professionals.

LOA

221 Camp St. • (504) 553-9550
www.ihhotel.com/loa/idea
HOURS 4 p.m–11 p.m. 7 days a week
NO HAPPY HOUR

Loa are the spirits of Haitian Voodoo. They are kind of like Catholic saints, serving as intermediaries between humans and the Creator. Each has his or her own personality, chants and songs, likes and dislikes. Taken as a whole, however, they form a harmonious group that intercedes between heaven and earth. Loa the bar is also a mixture of styles and personalities that also mesh together into a beautiful, even spiritually cohesive whole. The bar itself, located in the back of the space, is a kind of altar, covered in statues of holy figures that traverse religions. There's Buddha next to the Virgin Mary, who sits across from a Greek god. This aesthetic hodgepodge echoes throughout the space and produces an effect that my friend Allison described as "Louis XVI meets Pottery Barn." The glassware is equally mismatched, though consistently lovely, and all of it feels borrowed (stolen?) from someone's grandmother's china cabinet. Everyone looks good holding these glasses, especially when doing so in the soft glow of dozens of candles. The flickering gleam not only illuminates the patrons and statues but imbues the acolytes/bartenders with a somewhat holy air.

This mingling of seemingly incongruous elements is most fully realized in the cocktails served here. Alan Walter oversees the bar program, and his vision is one that is defined by exploration and experimentation. Loa offers one of the most thoughtful cocktail programs in the city. The flavor combinations are adventurous, often pushing the envelope of what might work together, but they never feel haphazard. Many of the ingredients are made or infused in-house, often utilizing herbs from Alan's garden. The bar is rarely busy, which means that bartenders have time to chat with you, making suggestions or explaining ingredients. If you are a solo traveler and want

Fresh herbs for drinks at Loa

to learn about your drink, it's a good place to be. If you are out with some-one special, though, or even a good friend with whom you need to catch up, Loa also fits the bill. The lighting is muted, and the sofas are plush and far enough apart so that you are never on top of another duo. It's a place that encourages you to slow down, which, in this 24/7 bustling world, is one of the most sacred acts I can think of.

RUSTY NAIL

1100 Constance St. • (504) 525-5515
www.therustynail.biz
HOURS 4 p.m.–1 a.m. Mon–Thu; 2 p.m.–3 a.m. Fri; noon–3 a.m. Sat;
noon–1 a.m. Sun
HAPPY HOUR Mon–Wed and Fri 4 p.m.–7 p.m.
Each Thursday they donate 20 percent of sales to a different non-profit in their Cocktails for a Cause series

Some bars are notable for their history. Others for lush surroundings. Still others gain fame because of carefully crafted drinks. The element that most defines a neighborhood bar is the people who go there and the relationships formed there. For many, the people at your local bar become another kind of family. In visiting the Rusty Nail recently, my friend Erica pointed out an example of this connection. One of the Nail's regulars is Frank. I learned that Frank used to come here with his elderly dog, Omar. Omar even had his own dog bed near the bar, where he would curl up and sleep as Frank chatted with patrons. When Omar died, The Rusty Nail put a tribute to the dog on their Facebook page, and customers posted their condolences. Today, Frank gingerly balanced a sleeping puppy on his shoulder as he sipped his glass of merlot. Frank's new puppy, Louie, was being trained in proper bar behavior (sleeping and not causing trouble), and patrons would occasionally come by and pat his head, with the familiarity of family.

In addition to these connections, what draws Erica back to the Nail (and what I also appreciate) is that no matter what you are in the mood to drink, you can get it. The rotating beer taps feature local and regional brews. The recently updated cocktail menu offers drinks with bitters made in-house. And unlike most neighborhood bars, the Nail has an admirable wine list.

Then, of course, there's the back patio. Unlike less manicured court-

The front entrance to the Rusty Nail

yards in New Orleans, the paving here is even, none of the chairs are broken, and large fans are strategically placed to keep things cool, even on a sweltering summer night. Three TVs offer patrons easy viewing of football, NBA playoffs, or, tonight, college baseball. Also, this evening, the Swampy Science Club has set up in the back, offering a free lecture on particle waves (always easier to understand when drinking). The Rusty Nail often hosts organizations and charity events in addition to trivia nights.

My favorite part of the bar, though, is one most folks might not notice. On a wall off to the side, near a section of the beer taps, is a gallery of photos. Some are of the family who owns the bar, some are bartenders, some are patrons. It is not a huge section, not in the way that some bars absolutely cover a wall with snapshots. Instead it is more like the refrigerator in your kitchen, with its collage of images of friends and family. Unlike at so many bars, where every component of your experience is curated, this provided a nice view into a personal moment for the employees. If you are at the Convention Center, the Rusty Nail is a mere three blocks away. Well worth a stop.

Historic murals at the Sazerac Bar

SAZERAC BAR

130 Roosevelt Way • (504) 648-1200

www.therooseveltneworleans.com/dining/the-sazerac-bar.html

HOURS 11 a.m.–2 a.m. 7 days a week

NO HAPPY HOUR

I've gotten a lot of good advice from my mother about what to drink and how to drink. Drink the good stuff, not too much. When you drink with friends, make sure to buy a round. Tip generously. She also taught me to appreciate a well-made drink in an old hotel bar. Few saloons in New Orleans fill this bill like the Sazerac Bar, which has all my mother's favorite bells and whistles.

Storied past? Check. Famous drinks like the Sazerac cocktail and Ramos Gin Fizz were invented or rediscovered here. Storied location? Check. It's in the Roosevelt Hotel, a venerable institution whose gilded lobby has welcomed stars from near and far including bon vivant and governor Huey P. Long. Look for the plaque recounting the story of Long's black bank box, supposedly stored at the hotel, which disappeared after his assassination. Beautiful decor? Check. The lounge boasts historic W.P.A.-era murals, a sweeping, polished wooden bar, and capacious leather sofas and chairs all waiting for your company.

The Sazerac can fill up in the evenings, so I try to hit it in the late afternoon, when there is plenty of seating. Table service means you don't have to worry about elbowing your way to the bar to order, but if there is room there, it's worth taking a seat there to enjoy the show. Bustling bartenders in crisp white jackets measure, shake, and pour. You probably won't be able to keep yourself from ordering house specialties like the Sazerac and Ramos Gin Fizz, but it's worth perusing their menu and trying one of the rotating seasonal options. Give yourself plenty of time to drink here: at least two rounds. By then you will have settled into your spot and easily forgotten whatever troubles may lie outside the sturdy walls of the hotel. It's why my mother loves hotel bars: you are guaranteed to be well tended to there. A friend once compared the Sazerac Bar to a nineteenth-century ocean liner. Amid the wooden paneled walls and covered ceilings, it's easy to imagine you are sailing the Atlantic on the QEII instead of sailing to better times on waves of whiskey.

SWIZZLE STICK

300 Poydras St. • (504) 595-3305
www.cafeadelaide.com
HOURS 11 a.m.–midnight 7 days a week
HAPPY HOUR 3 p.m.–6 p.m.

Cafe Adelaide's proprietors are Ti Martin and Lally Brennan, members of the Brennan restaurateur clan. They named the restaurant and bar in honor of their favorite aunt, Adelaide—a New Orleans character if there ever was one—who owned a blue fur, a pink fur, a mink, a sable, and finally a monkey coat with a matching hat. She also (allegedly) always wore a gold swizzle stick on a chain around her neck, keeping it handy in case her drink ever needed an extra stir. Apparently it was used frequently and with relish. Their signature drink, The Adelaide Swizzle, is named in her honor and made with dark rum and a secret ingredient. The atmosphere of the bar reflects that sense of bonhomie. The menu changes with the seasons, but standards anchor it, as is typical of a classic New Orleans restaurant.

Though I love sitting at the bar and watching bartenders carve ice cubes

Good times at the Swizzle Stick Bar

from the ice block centerpiece, I also like to take my drink into the hotel lobby. The cushiony sofas and chairs and big window on to Poydras offer a great spot in the Central Business District for people watching while sipping a well-crafted drink in swank surroundings.

W.I.N.O.(WINE INSTITUTE OF NEW ORLEANS)

610 Tchoupitoulas St. • (504) 324-8000

www.winoschool.com

HOURS 2 p.m.–10 p.m. Sun–Weds; 2 p.m.–midnight Thu–Sat

HAPPY HOUR 5 p.m.–7 p.m. Mon–Wed; 9 p.m.–midnight Thu–Sun

While I can enjoy pretty much any whiskey you sit in front of me, finding a wine I really love is more of a challenge. I know which styles I prefer and do my best to articulate those flavors, but you can only get so far with "raisins and tobacco," and I often find myself drinking a glass of something too dry or too sweet, feeling like the Goldilocks of wine, pining for something "just right." Whenever possible, to help narrow the field, I ask (politely) for a small pour of two wines. If I don't really like either of them, I either stick with liquor or end up choosing the least offensive option. I mean, I can't keep drinking samples all night, hoping I find the perfect pour, right? I can't, that is, unless I go to W.I.N.O.

W.I.N.O. stocks more than 120 bottles of wine, each kept on tap in a special (magical?) machine, so it never spoils. The machines and bottles dominate the space, and as a fan of decorating with alcohol (see Capdeville), I am charmed. The bar is self-serve—like fro-yo, but better. In exchange for your driver's license or other I.D., you receive a "tasting card" which you insert into the machine to activate its wine dispenser. You choose a one, two or four-ounce pour, and prices for each are listed above the dispensing button. One of my favorite aspects of this whole oenophilic experience is that it's not cheaper by the ounce to serve a larger pour. You aren't penalized for only having a taste. A card with a description of the wine, along with a pithy phrase summarizing its character, is perched above each bottle. A big Amarone, for example, is called "My Cousin Vinny."

The space at W.I.N.O. is lovely old brick and was once clearly part of a larger warehouse. Make sure to visit the back room, which houses tables for larger parties as well as sweeter white wines. There's nowhere else quite like W.I.N.O in New Orleans and I tip my hat to owner Bryan Burkey, who brought this concept to the city. At W.I.N.O. I never have to worry about pestering a server for "just a taste," and I never have to worry about drinking a glass of something that is just OK. Theoretically I could try a one-ounce pour of every single wine in this bar. I probably shouldn't, but I could.

CHAPTER 6

Garden District

After the signing of the Louisiana Purchase, Americans flocked to New Orleans in droves seeking land and opportunity. The local French-speaking Catholics did not welcome these English-speaking Protestants, so instead of settling in the already developed French Quarter, they moved across Canal Street and created a newer, American section of town. There was a lot of political bickering between the French Creoles and the Americans, so from 1836 to 1853, the city was actually split into three municipalities, each with its own separate government but beholden to one mayor and a City Council composed of representatives from each of the three sections. The French Quarter was one municipality, the Marigny and Bywater occupied another, and much of what is now the rest of New Orleans occupied a third, named Sainte Marie/Saint Mary.

Saint Mary Street lies in the Lower Garden District, and it is here you begin to see a significant difference in architecture from the houses on the other side of Canal Street. The Garden District was a home away from home for many of the sugar planters whose plantations lined the Mississippi River. They would come to New Orleans to conduct business, and once a year they would bring their families to participate in society balls held during the Carnival season. Many of their homes still stand and are best viewed while sipping something delicious while riding the St. Charles Streetcar.

THE AVENUE PUB

1732 St. Charles Ave. • (504) 586-9243
theavenuepub.com
HOURS 24 hours 7 days a week
HAPPY HOUR 4 p.m.–6 p.m. Mon–Fri

The Avenue Pub is the premier beer bar in New Orleans and one of the best in the region. That alone is reason enough for any beer fan to visit this mecca for brew. But even if beer isn't your thing, it's still worth going to this 24-hour neighborhood joint—it pours as robust a whiskey list as any in the city, and its bartenders are friendly to beer nerds and novices alike.

Until 2006, the Avenue Pub was a typical neighborhood bar, pouring big-brand beer and basic booze at low prices. Then the owner died and his daughter, Polly Watts, took over. Over the next several years, she transformed the bar into a beer haven, one of the first in the city to focus on regional, national and international craft beers. The forty-plus taps change regularly and offer rare beers from around the world. Her strong

The Avenue Pub

relationships with brewers and distributors mean she carries beers that no one else in the city or even region may carry, including beers from Cantillon and De La Senne in Belgium. Visitors who have a hard time choosing from among the bounty can sample four-ounce servings, creating their own flights.

Before taking over her dad's pub, Polly lived in Louisville, Kentucky, and her whiskey list reflects the time she spent surrounded by America's spirit. While most neighborhood joints offer "programming" like trivia or movie nights, the Avenue Pub hosts regular visits from brewers, distillers, and other folks in the industry, who pour special barrels of whiskey or collaborations between several breweries. Although the bar's drink menu is upscale, the vibe is still very low-key. It is a 24-hour bar, after all, and drinking here at 3 a.m. comes with all the woozy delight that hour affords. That also means that bartenders here accept all kinds of drinkers, from someone who wants a pretty basic pilsner to someone who knows exactly what kind of glass his Imperial Stout should be served in. There are no snobs working at the Avenue Pub.

The upstairs bar opens at 5 p.m. daily and its balcony affords a lovely view of St. Charles Avenue. If you love beer or whiskey (or both) the Avenue Pub is a must-visit. I probably Uber home and leave my car parked here overnight more than any other bar in town, because once I start sampling, it's hard to stop. Each time I drink here, I learn something new about beer, and doing so while drinking on a balcony makes the learning even more fun. Given that my business is called Drink & Learn, it's not surprising that the Avenue Pub is one of my favorite bars in the city.

BALCONY BAR

3201 Magazine St. • (504) 895-1600
HOURS 4 p.m.–2 a.m. Mon–Thu; noon–3 a.m. Fri and Sat; noon–2 a.m. Sunday
HAPPY HOUR 4 p.m.–8 p.m. 7 days a week

This bar is huge. Head here if you are out with any kind of group, because even on a busy Saturday night, there will be room for all of you. You can hang out downstairs, among the booths and TVs, at the scruffy wooden bar that easily sits twenty. Or head upstairs and gather around the giant square

A bar full of whiskey at Barrel Proof

bar that dominates the room. But if the weather is nice, you should look for a spot among the dozen tables perched out on the balcony that gives the bar its name.

Unlike in the French Quarter, there aren't a lot of bars with balconies across Canal and even fewer that can accommodate many people. Here, you can peer down on Magazine Street, where car traffic slows considerably in the evenings and is eventually replaced by pedestrians moving from bar to restaurant to bar. The Balcony Bar is a neighborhood joint with a solid beer list and decent prices. Daily drink specials keep your wallet full, and the tasty Pirate Pizza served in the back kitchen does the same for your belly. On a recent visit, our bartender was friendly and committed to her craft, even in a spot that isn't exactly famous for cocktails. When my neighbor ordered a margarita, she hand-squeezed limes and oranges into the glass. When I asked her why, she remarked that while she hates sour mix, someone broke her juicer, and so she had been reduced to doctoring it up as best she could ever since. If I lived near here, I would drink here more.

BARREL PROOF

1201 Magazine St. • (504) 299-1888

www.barrelproofnola.com

HOURS 4 p.m.–1 a.m. Sun–Thu; 4 p.m.–2 a.m. Fri and Sat

HAPPY HOUR 4 p.m.–6 p.m. Mon–Fri

A "beer and a shot," is a favorite combination, especially among service workers after a long shift. Barrel Proof has organized its entire menu around this concept, offering a selection of more than sixty brews and two hundred whiskeys to mix and match.

The cavernous space has walls covered with corrugated sheet metal, which feels more West Texas than New Orleans. Taxidermied animals peer down at patrons sipping along the forty-four-foot bar, an altar to whiskey. Glancing at the menu, you might think that all they serve is beer and whiskey. Page after page lists brown liquor and brew. When I asked the bartender if that was the case, he laughed, shook his head, and pointed to the menu's final page. The sum total of tequilas, vodkas, and rums listed there is less than the number of American bourbons available. You don't go to Barrel Proof for the rum.

The menu is immense, organized by country of origin, with a brief description of each whiskey's mash bills and aging process. You can order your whiskey in one-ounce or two-ounce pours. The cost per ounce doesn't change, so you can't use the argument "It's cheaper to get two ounces" to talk yourself into a larger pour, as I admit to often doing. In addition to offering some rare American bourbons, they also carry all of the Japanese whiskeys available in Louisiana. While you can choose themed whiskey flights, the one-ounce pours also make it easy for patrons to design their own. The opportunity to try some high-end whiskeys without emptying your wallet is appealing, but so is the option of drinking on the cheap. Barrel Proof offers the whole spectrum of drinking, from downing the $5 Schlitz and Old Grand-Dad to spending $30 on a Japanese import. Craving a traditional daiquiri or Last Word? Fear not. The bartenders are talented and can mix up traditional cocktails, in addition to doling out whiskey and beer advice.

The vibe is decidedly informal, a tone set by the friendly and helpful staff, who are happy to help you decide where to start and, occasionally, where to end. Traveling with a big group? Barrel Proof is spacious enough for large parties to spread out. The crowd is usually pretty mixed as well, and the last time I was there I saw several couples who were clearly on dates as well as a group of boisterous, highly groomed young men celebrating a friend's birthday, all sporting rainbow and unicorn t-shirts that declared, "I'm totally straight." Just like my whiskey.

BAYOU BAR AT THE PONTCHARTRAIN HOTEL

2031 St. Charles Ave. • (504) 323-1456
www.bayoubarneworleans.com
HOURS 11 a.m.–11 p.m. Sun–Thu; 11 a.m.–midnight Fri and Sat
NO HAPPY HOUR

The Pontchartrain Hotel originally opened as an apartment building in 1927, but it found its feet in the 1940s, when it transformed into a luxury hotel. In the 1950s and 1960s it hosted a "who's who" list that included Frank Sinatra, Rita Hayworth, and multiple presidents. Jim Morrison and the Doors stayed there in 1970 after performing their last concert ever. The hotel became a little down-at-heel, particularly after Hurricane Katrina, and its 2016 renovation was highly anticipated by locals with fond memories of dining in the lush Caribbean Room or drinking in the bar to the sounds of pianist extraordinaire Phil Melancon. Not only have the new owners restored the venerable old hotel, they have refurbished the bar and renamed it the Bayou Bar. More importantly, they have brought back Mr. Melancon, who still tickles the ivories each weekend. Fortunately for us, the gorgeous marshland mural that has decorated the space since the 1940s is still there, augmented by a rustic cypress bar. Patrons can sip from a number of whiskeys or try some of the signature cocktails, all named for local favorite spots like the Dorignac 75 (a locally owned grocery store) and the Palmer Park Swizzle (a park just down the street). I love, love, love the pass-through window connecting the bar to the hotel's lounge, where you can sip your cocktail among a gallery of paintings while lazing on your choice of divans, chaise lounges, and ottomans galore.

When you tire of that opulence, make your way to the Hot Tin rooftop bar, one of many new places offering views of the city. The spacious bar's decor is inspired by Tennessee Williams, who worked on *A Streetcar Named Desire* while staying at the Pontchartrain in the 1940s. The room feels a bit like a hipster TGIFridays: statues, photos, books, and memorabilia cover the walls, spill from cabinets, and overflow from desks. Patrons are welcome to sit in rattan chairs and thumb through the collection, and it's certainly a welcome way to pass the time while sipping on an Old Fashioned. But don't forget to step outside, no matter the heat, and take in the spectacular view of the Crescent City connection.

The Pontchartrain Hotel is one of New Orleans's treasures. Despite the recent renovation, this place still feels old, like the grand dame it was. Take the streetcar here and raise a glass to Mr. Williams, a man who aptly observed in the play he penned here, "Liquor sure goes fast in hot weather."

THE BULLDOG

3236 Magazine St. • (504) 891-1516
www.thebulldoguptown.com
HOURS 11 a.m.–2 a.m. 7 days a week
HAPPY HOUR 3 p.m.–6 p.m.

Open the cabinet of most New Orleanians under thirty and you will probably see a pint glass from the Bulldog. No, it's not stolen. On Wednesdays at the Bulldog, your pint glass is free with purchase. For millennials who would rather spend their meager earnings on beer instead of glassware, it's the perfect way to stock your cabinets. This dog-friendly spot is beloved by beer fans, who come to enjoy the lively courtyard with a back wall that sports a "beer taps fountain"—unfortunately, it only pours water. Inside, the bar has almost fifty taps and more than one hundred bottles of local, regional, and national beers, and the Bulldog is regularly near the top of New Orleanians' list of favorite beer bars. The courtyard and rather small bar both fill up quickly, especially during football season. Fans of teams not in the SEC might want to steer clear on Saturdays, when the several TVs are tuned solely to games south of the Mason-Dixon line. The atmosphere then can feel a little "bro-ey," but on weeknights the crowd is more varied, as folks stop in for an after-work beer. Though this bar may seem casual, it takes its beer very seriously, regularly cleaning out its lines and changing beers often. They take the same pride in their food, which is one of the better bets for late-night fare. The Bulldog is one of the few bars in town that sells growlers, and if you are staying nearby, it's a good place to fill up a jug with a craft brew to enjoy if the place is too full.

Polly Watts

Polly Watts may not have always planned to run a bar. But when she took over the Avenue Pub in 2006, she decided not only to make it a great, 24-hour neighborhood bar, but also to make it one of the premier beer bars in the region. The Avenue Pub belonged to Polly's father from 1987 to 2006, when he passed away. She envisioned the bar as a hub for craft beer and quality whiskey, neither of which was really present in New Orleans at that time.

For the first two years of her tenure, she had difficulty sourcing the beers she wanted for her menu. Once, in order to get a distributor to give her one keg of a particular Imperial IPA, she had to agree to take a whole pallet, ten kegs. This was more beer than she would ever normally have purchased of such a specialized style, but Polly decided to take a risk in order to create the kind of beer bar that fit her vision. She told the distributor, "OK, I'll take them all." And then she sold them all.

Polly continued to hit barriers in trying to build her bar, but she kept finding ways to move closer to her vision. "I don't take the word 'no' very well," she admits. She credits the strong relationships she has formed as vital to the development of her bar. "The craft beer community is great for sharing advice. A brewery can be your supplier or they can be your community. I made a lot of friends. That helped." Watts also credits other New Orleans bars that were pouring quality brews before she did as helping to pave her way. "I wouldn't have been able to do it without Cooter Brown's, DBA, and The Bulldog. They laid the groundwork." The Avenue Pub now has several different reputations: beer bar, whiskey bar, neighborhood bar. And it is, after all, still a 24-hour bar, with all that entails. When Watts pauses to look back on the last ten years, she says, "Damn, I really did do a lot." Grateful beer lovers across the city agree.

HALF MOON BAR & GRILL

1125 St. Mary St. • (504) 593-0011

www.halfmoongrillnola.com

HOURS noon–4 a.m. 7 days a week

HAPPY HOUR 5 p.m.–8 p.m. 7 days a week

The Half Moon straddles the line between neighborhood bar and dive. It's dark and just a little grimy, like a dive, with a friendly rapport between the bartenders and customers, like a neighborhood bar. The bar is stocked with regulars whose drinks the bartenders call out as they sit down. We hear the bartender call out, "Crown and Coke?" to one man who nods and settles onto a stool to watch basketball playoffs. The rotating list of drink specials means you can get a drink for $3 or less any night of the week. The abundance of TVs keeps sports fans happy. The pool table, dartboards, and skee-ball table all lend themselves to groups gathered in friendly competition and are good places to meet locals. The Half Moon can get downright rowdy when it is packed, as it often is during football games and weekend nights. Though the bar is spacious, the crowd often overflows into the back courtyard, sipping their $3 Pabst longnecks. Come on a weeknight to drink with regulars and practice your skee-ball technique, all for under $10.

THE SAINT

961 St. Mary St. • (504) 523-0050

www.thesaintneworleans.com

HOURS 3 p.m.–til 7 days a week

NO HAPPY HOUR

There was time when I was on a streak with the Saint. Every time I went there (OK, like three or four times, but in a row), someone took their clothes off in the photo booth. The streak ended a while back, but each time I visit the Saint, I still kind of hope for a show. In its absence, I turn to the bar, another kind of show. Tuesdays are Tikioki, a perfect concoction of tiki-fueled karaoke performances. Thursday "After Dark, My Sweet" movie nights feature crime and noir films, free popcorn, and $2 Tecates. Weekend night soundtracks come from DJs, and Sundays get turned over to the crowd via

Free Jukebox night. The jukebox at the Saint is a delight. Lee Dorsey shares a page with the Dead Milkmen, the New York Dolls, and Jacques Dutronc.

The Saint is pretty tiny for all its wonder, and though there is a patio out back, I've never taken my drink there. I like to hunker down at the bar, watch whoever and whatever comes out of the photo booth, visit with the bartender and whomever I find at the adjacent barstool. For a while, Sean Yseult, founder of White Zombie, owned and ran the bar, and it carries with it that punk/metal feel. The crowd here can definitely skew a little dark and goth, and most are pretty inked-up, though if you come in wearing a pink sundress, as I have, no one cares.

THE TASTING ROOM

1906 Magazine St. • (504) 581-3880
www.ttrneworleans.com
HOURS 3 p.m.–11 p.m. Tue–Sun
HAPPY HOUR (Leisure Hour) 4 p.m.–6 p.m. daily, and all day Wed

The Tasting Room was opened by two California transplants, Toby and Lisa Devore, who moved to New Orleans and brought with them their love of good wine. It is truly a bar for oenophiles, with a thoughtfully curated wine list served in an elegant setting. The old-world feel of the space is an interesting mix of rustic refinement, and the exposed brick offers an unpolished contrast to the elegant chandeliers. Velvet chairs and leather couches call to patrons to relax and enjoy the hundreds of wines available (by the glass or bottle) while listening to the music that is never too loud to impede conversation, even when the Spanish guitar player regales patrons with his dexterous playing on Thursday nights. Curious patrons can sample $20 themed tastings or put themselves in the capable hands of a very knowledgeable staff. The wine menu is a bit pricey, with quite a few bottles over $100 and few wines by the glass under $10. But the stylish atmosphere makes it worth the rent on the chair.

The neat patio is covered, so one can sit out here in summer evenings enjoying classic movies like *Casablanca* projected on the brick wall. Though located on trendy Magazine Street, the Tasting Room never feels like it's part of the "scene." Instead, it feels intimate, and even when it fills up, the spacious room seems to expand to accommodate the crowd. I went to the

Tasting Room with two wine lovers, neither of whom had been there before. Both made plans to return the following week, and did. As we polished off the last of several flights and sank back into the velvet chairs to regroup, one of them observed, "This is a really nice way to spend the night." It is indeed.

TRACEY'S

2604 Magazine St. • (504) 897-5413
www.traceysnola.com
HOURS 11 a.m.–til 7 days a week
HAPPY HOUR 4 p.m.–7 p.m. Mon–Fri

Here's what you need to know about Tracey's. The owner, Jeffrey Carreras, ran a New Orleans institution, Parasols, for twelve years. Then the building Parasols was housed in got bought by some folks from Florida, and Jeff was kicked out. Jeff left Parasol's (taking the staff, decorations and secret roast beef po' boy recipe with him), bought a much larger building one block from his old digs, and then opened a new bar three days later. This new building used to be a bar, Tracey's, and Jeff decided to honor its heritage by keeping the old name. That was in 2010. It's been going gangbusters ever since. Tracey's is a great neighborhood sports bar. If you are looking for a place to watch college or NFL football, this is the spot. But come early, or you will be peering through the windows to get a view of the screen. I once came here for a Saints game, and the bar was three deep. When I ordered a pitcher of beer, the bartender made me swear to return soon, saying, "Please bring it back. It's my last one." While most of the twenty TVs were tuned to the Saints game, a few screens showed matchups from across the league. These TVs served as hubs for their fans. Everyone is welcome at Tracey's, even Atlanta fans.

Tracey's decor features the ubiquitous signs for beer and liquor. The one incongruous element is the several dozen green parasols hanging from the ceiling. Decorated with feathers and glitter, they gently sway above the crowd. While Tracey's is a great bar no matter the day, it really comes into its own on game day. And nowhere else but Tracey's offers this kind of celebration under the benevolent shade of a dozen green parasols.

CHAPTER 7

Uptown

Though some may argue about where the boundary lies between Uptown and the Garden District, no one can argue that one of the defining features of this section of town is Audubon Park. Though not nearly as large as City Park in Mid-City, Audubon is a charming place to take a stroll, especially if it takes you to the end nearest Magazine Street and into the Audubon Zoo. Audubon Park was once part of a plantation owned by Etienne Bore, the man who first granulated sugar on a commercial scale. It's appropriate that the source of the city's wealth (at least in the nineteenth century) started in the city's neighborhood most associated with wealth. Rich folks live everywhere in New Orleans, but there seems to be a higher concentration of them here, and many of the bars in this area are quite swanky. Loyola and Tulane Universities are also in Uptown, which means there is a proliferation of college bars geared to their students, none of which are in this book.

ALINE STREET BEER GARDEN/GARDEN DISTRICT

1515 Aline St. • (504) 891-5774
www.facebook.com/AlineStreetBeerGarden
HOURS 4 p.m.–midnight Mon–Thu; 2 p.m.–2 a.m. Fri; 11 a.m.–2 a.m. Sat and Sun

People love to drink out of unusually shaped vessels. It's a quirk of humanity that French Quarter merchants exploit, offering Bourbon Street imbibers plastic hand grenades, footballs, jesters and more from which to sip. While most bars in the rest of the city eschew this cheeky service, Aline

Street Beer Garden has embraced it, offering those who order a pitcher of beer something a little more interesting: a boot. When I visited the bar on a Tuesday night (Boot Night!) both the picnic tables outside and the bar inside were dotted with plastic footwear filled with German beer. Here, Aventinus and Spaten Lager are always on tap alongside local brews including Bayou Teche, Covington, and Parish Breweries. The bottle selection sports a wide variety of classic German brews like Warsteiner and Spaten Optimator. All are perfect for washing down a rotating series of pop-up kitchens serving sliders, pizza and cheesesteaks. The beer focus echoes in the drink specials: In addition to Tuesday boot night, Thursday is cask night, with pours from local brewers. Bartender Adam notes that Boot Night offers patrons one of the cheapest pitchers in the city, $14.75 for two liters of most of their draft beers (fancier beers can run more). Even if you aren't there on Tuesday, you can still get a boot for $19.75. The picnic tables don't exactly constitute a "beer garden," but they expand the reach of this narrow spot. And hockey fans, take note: Aline Street Beer Garden also bills itself as a hockey bar and is a perfect spot for devotees to cheer (or cry) in their boots.

BOULIGNY TAVERN

3641 Magazine St. • (504) 891-1810

www.boulignytavern.com

HOURS 4 p.m.–midnight Mon–Thu; 4 p.m.–2 a.m. Fri and Sat

HAPPY HOUR 4 p.m.–6 p.m. Mon–Thu

I've been meeting friends for drinks at Bouligny Tavern for years, but until I wrote this book, I had always done my drinking here near the end of the evening, when my booze-blurred eyesight was probably not helped by the dim lighting. Until I came during the day, I never really appreciated what a visually appealing spot the Bouligny Tavern is. Their website describes the vibe as "your father's den with your grandparents' furniture and your cool uncle's record collection," which is spot on. The furniture is an eclectic mix of *Mad Men* castoffs, a little scruffy but in a comfortable way. Sunburst lamps adorn the walls, and patrons lounge on banquettes under the rays of a star-shaped chandelier. Or at least they can "lounge" during happy hour. If you come here at night, the crowd fills the room, and you would be lucky to make eye contact with a server, much less find a seat. But today, the room is empty, save for a few drinkers at the bar seated on Marcel Breuer barstools. A record player sits behind the bar with stacks of vintage vinyl propped against it. The exhortations of Nancy Sinatra fill the room and by my second drink I am in total accord with her that my boots are indeed made for walking, though maybe not just yet. Though I choose to stay inside and enjoy the 1960s vibe, the heated patio with its couches (more lounging!) calls my name, even on this chilly winter day. Bouligny Tavern is my new favorite Uptown happy hour. The discounted snacks prepared under the eagle eyes of famed Chef John Harris of Lilette are enough to merit the trek Uptown. My bartender also served me a daiquiri that can stand alongside anything the craft rum bars in the Quarter are serving. I'll be crossing Canal to visit Bouligny Tavern again soon.

CAVAN

3607 Magazine St. • (504) 509-7655
www.cavannola.com
HOURS 5 p.m.–10 p.m. Mon–Thu; 10:30 a.m.–11 p.m. Fri–Sun
HAPPY HOUR 4 p.m.–6 p.m. Mon–Fri

Drinking at Cavan is a good way to get a glimpse of what it was like to visit a home along Magazine in the eighteenth century. Unlike many houses in the city that were converted to commercial spaces—where you can just barely make out the bones of what was a residence—Cavan still feels like a home. Original chandeliers hang from the ceilings, and though the original molding was too damaged to salvage, the owners have carefully preserved the sensibility of the 1881 property.

The upstairs bar is full of rosy hues, and the pressed-tin ceiling keeps the room feeling historic and warm. As Matt, the bar manager, put it, "We want it to feel like you are visiting your grandmother's house." Apparently, it's a grandmother who knows how to make a mean drink. My go-to drink there is the Alabazam, a riff on the Sidecar, enhanced with bitters. The inspiration for the restaurant's name came from owner Robert LeBlanc's grandfather, who arrived in New Orleans from County Cavan, Ireland at age eight and grew up just a few blocks away.

Upstairs bar at Cavan

If it's a nice day, you can also sit outside, but I prefer the upstairs bar, where I can nosh on Cavan's complimentary, homemade oyster crackers. They are a gesture of Cavan's signature hospitality, and they make my cocktail even tastier.

CLUB MS. MAE'S

4336 Magazine St. • (504) 218-8035

www.msmaeswallofshame.blogspot.com (This is not the website for the bar, but a website chronicling bad decisions made there. The actual bar has no website.)

HOURS 24 hours a day 7 days a week
NO HAPPY HOUR

Until I had to write this book, I had never been to Ms. Mae's sober. And even for this book, I wasn't entirely sober. No one should ever go to Ms. Mae's completely sober. Instead, Ms Mae's is where the night ends, perhaps even long after it should have ended. All of my visits there are tinged with a haze, and my memories are foggy at best. This visit was meant to confirm vague beliefs about what actually happens in this bar. Here is what was confirmed:

1. Don't go sober. Ms. Mae's is a dive. It is dark, and it appears dirtier than it probably is. The cement floor looks perfect for hosing off, and the space itself feels like it was abandoned, then found and turned into a bar. But you aren't coming for the decor. You are coming because of Observation #2.

2. Ms. Mae's is extraordinarily cheap. A shot of well alcohol will set you back $2, while a nice pour of a double puts you back $3. Call brands such as Jim Beam run $3. Beers are similarly priced: PBR and Highlife are $2, and Abita is $3.

3. Ms. Mae's is cash only. There is an ATM if your wallet has less than $5, which is all you need unless you are buying a round for 3 people or more.

4. Ms. Mae's is 24 hours. If you forget this, step outside and read the hand-painted sign that fills the building's exterior wall.

5. If you need something to do here besides drink (and really, do you need to be doing anything else?) you can amuse yourself playing video golf, air hockey, and of course, video poker.

6. You're probably not going to begin your drinking here, unless that drinking starts at noon. Or earlier.

But it sure is a great place to end your drinking. If it's 3 a.m., you are so not done, and you are already Uptown, then Ms. Mae's has got your name all over it, though you really don't want your name recorded here, because that means you ended up on their Wall of Shame.

COLUMNS HOTEL VICTORIAN LOUNGE
3811 St. Charles Ave. • (504) 899-9308
www.thecolumns.com/#!the-victorian-lounge
HOURS 3 p.m.–midnight Mon–Thu; noon–midnight Fri–Sun
HAPPY HOUR 5 p.m.–7 p.m. 7 days a week

While New Orleans was colonized by the French, it didn't reach its apogee of wealth until the arrival of sugar cultivation in the early 1800s. A combination of joining the United States (via the Louisiana Purchase), getting into the business of sugar production, and then being the sole provider of that "white gold" led to the city's wealth. During that time, scores of Americans arrived, seeking fortune. Those who succeeded built houses—mansions, really—in the developing American sector. The Columns was built for Simon Hernsheim, owner of Hernsheim Brothers and Co., the largest manufacturer of cigars in the United States in the late nineteenth century. The house is a well-preserved piece of nineteenth-century grandeur and was the set for the film *Pretty Baby*, a terrible movie about the prostitutes of Storyville and E.J. Bellocq, who photographed them.

Drinking at the Columns is a really sweet deal. For the price of a drink you get to spend an hour or more in the middle of nineteenth-century splendor.

If the Victorian lounge is crowded (and frankly, it often is), you can take your drink into the adjoining parlors, which often feature live music. The Columns is a favorite bar of Tulane law students. When you tire of discussions of constitutional law, head to the front porch, snag a table with a view of lovely St. Charles Avenue. Watch the streetcars come trundling by and pretend for a moment you are Mr. Hernsheim. Hell, go ahead and light a cigar. You are outside, after all.

DELACHAISE

3442 St. Charles Ave. • (504) 895-0858
www.thedelachaise.com
HOURS 5 p.m.–til Mon-Thu; 3 p.m.–til Fri–Sun
NO HAPPY HOUR

Some people's image of a wine bar is that of a quiet, staid, formal place where everyone sits around talking about tannins. At Delachaise, you are lucky if your friends can hear you talk about anything above the noise of this lively, popular spot. The Delachaise offers the largest selection of wines by the glass in New Orleans, ranging in price from $7 to $60, with happy hour prices often dipping to $5 a glass. Though this galley of a bar can get absolutely packed in the evening, when the crowds thin, it's lovely to sit at the Prytania Street end of the bar and look down toward St. Charles Avenue, where tipsy patrons congregate under Christmas lights chatting about anything but aroma or acidity.

Don't come here seeking lots of wine advice. The bartenders are amiable and knowledgeable but are often too swamped to offer more than a cursory opinion on the difference between one Malbec and another. The Delachaise sits along St. Charles Avenue, and its bistro tables along the streetcar route often fill up when the weather is nice. But I prefer the din and merriment inside, a little bit of Montmarte found in Uptown.

DOS JEFES

5535 Tchoupitoulas St. • (504) 891-8500
www.dosjefes.com
HOURS 5 p.m.–til 7 days a week
HAPPY HOUR 5 p.m.–7 p.m. 7 days a week

Back in 2015, the New Orleans City Council passed a resolution banning smoking in all New Orleans bars. For some it was a death knell; others were more sanguine about the matter. Six months into the ban, a reporter interviewed bar owners and heard similar mixed reactions: some had observed a distinct slack in business, others not so much. There was a type of bar that definitely felt an uptick, whose business allowed at least one kind of smoking: cigars. Dos Jefes and a few other cigar bars were allowed to permit cigar smoking in their establishments. I had not been to Dos Jefes since the ban went into effect, and frankly I had not realized just how used to non-smoking I had become. If you go to Dos Jefes, be prepared: It is smoky, and not just a little. You can escape to the charming patio if you need a break (an irony, since the patio is the only place where smokers at other bars can go these days) but a heavy thunderstorm kept us inside. The air was thick with clouds of cigar smoke, and the pungent aroma was cut by another kind of smokiness: Scotch. Dos Jefe's is a cigar and whiskey bar, specifically a Scotch whisky bar, and fans of that island's creation can choose from a long list of its spirits. The decor matches the theme: Photographs of celebrities smoking cigars line the walls alongside numerous whiskey barrel tops.

Though not everyone there was smoking, most were. The room filled and the crowd got lively, especially once Joe Krown showed up to play his weekly set in this last bastion of a smoky New Orleans bar. Everyone settled in with their smokiness of choice: cigars, Scotch, or both.

FAT HARRY'S

4330 St. Charles Ave. • (504) 895-9582
No website
HOURS 10 a.m.–2 a.m. 7 days a week
HAPPY HOUR 4 p.m.–7 p.m.

When Carl Huling, the owner of Fat Harry's, passed away in February of 2010, the *Times-Picayune* penned a thoughtful tribute to the beloved owner. Former employees and current patrons added notes of condolence in the comments section. One man noted, "So sad. Fat Harry's was one of the first to open their doors after Katrina and the Federal Flood. They fed us, got us drunk, listened to our stories and we listened to theirs. Fat Harry's became an oasis in a sea of confusion." This sentiment echoes that of Fat Harry's fans, many of whom think of Fat Harry's as an extension of their living rooms.

The bar was opened by in 1970 by Allen Ignatius Boudreaux Jr., a member of the Phi Kappa Theta fraternity at Loyola University, and for years the bar catered primarily to that university crowd. But unlike some college bars, whose patrons often leave their college watering holes once they graduate, Fat Harry's has a strong pull. Patrons returned to enter its arched, church-like wooden doors and drink inside its hallowed walls, no matter their academic status. The bar's following grew and now Fat Harry's is an Uptown mainstay. Patrons line up along the copper-topped bar, whose dings and dents attest to extensive use. Their ages range from barely-21-year-olds to seersucker-sporting attorneys who crossed fifty many years ago. A decent wine list keeps older ladies clustered at one end of the bar happy. At the other end, several younger women sip Palomas and flirt with a group of guys who finish one pitcher and call for another. Like many bars in the city, Fat Harry's is a Saints and LSU hub, but it also caters to Clemson and University of Kentucky alumni, and flags for these schools hang in the back room by the pool table. I have a soft spot for a claw machine game, especially the one at Fat Harry's, with slightly naughty toys mixed among the plush animals. Most locals end up at Fat Harry's at least once during Carnival. Many

Uptown parades start near there, and it's a handy spot to pop in for a drink. But Fat Harry's is better enjoyed when you aren't pushing through throngs of revelers and when you have time to hang with friends in a place that feels like home.

HENRY'S

5101 Magazine St. • (504) 324-8140
www.henrysbaruptown.com
HOURS 3 p.m.–til Mon–Wed; 1 p.m.–til Thu and Fri; 10:30 a.m.–til Sat; 10 a.m.–til Sun
HAPPY HOUR Open til 7 p.m. Tue–Fri

They really don't make 'em like Henry's anymore, mainly because Henry's Uptown Bar was made in 1900. Henry's is the fourth oldest bar in New Orleans and the oldest outside of downtown. Opened by Irish immigrants James Lee and Margaret Tully Lee, Henry's Uptown Bar has remained under family ownership since its inception.

While a few neighborhood bars in New Orleans decorate their walls with political memorabilia from past decades, Henry's takes this practice to another level, and I have a particular fondness for their collection. The post announcing a rally for Earl K. Long always makes me smile. Like his older brother Huey, Earl Long was known for his political antics and insalubrious love life (he dated stripper Blaze Starr). He was governor twice, from 1948–52 and 1956–60, and he rankled many of the more conservative politicians, who attempted to oust him from office by declaring him mentally unfit to govern. Long savvily fired the director of all state mental hospitals, (which was in his power to do) and filled the position with a crony. He was then pronounced fit to remain.

Above Earl are portraits of Fats Domino (signed) and JFK (unsigned), holding equal prominence. Photos of the bar owners, their families, and patrons also pepper the walls, spanning the decades from the 1940s to the present. Requisite Saints paraphernalia abounds, and the *Times-Picayune* front page announcing their Super Bowl win hangs next to the *Times-Picayune* front page announcing the surrender of Germany in World War II. Interestingly, none of it feels haphazard or jumbled, and the room is not so full that you can't enjoy scanning it for the next new surprise.

Henry's is full of regulars whose ages, like the newspaper covers on display, span the decades. Thirty-somethings sip house-made sangria next to ladies "of a certain age" sipping Taaka and soda. It's a bar I would love to drink in with my mother; we would both feel equally at home. The drinks are cheap, the beers are cold, and the company is warm. After all, their slogan is "Serving beer before you were born," and they don't appear to be stopping anytime soon.

KENTON'S

5757 Magazine St. • (504) 891-1177
kentonsrestaurant.com
HOURS 3 p.m.–5:30 a.m. 7 days a week
HAPPY HOUR 3 p.m.–6 p.m. 7 days a week

One way to know how important a bar is to a restaurant is to look at how much space is allocated to drinking. At Kenton's, the whiskey-focused bar occupies almost half of the building's square footage. The drinks menu is dominated by America's favorite brown spirit, with categories including Whiskey Cocktails (Kenton's originals), Classic Whiskey Cocktails (Sazerac

Sipping whiskey at Kenton's

and Boulevardier), Whiskey Mixed Drinks (like the Spicy Buck: Rebel Yell and Blenheim's Spicy Ginger Ale) and finally Whiskey & A Beer (From Here to Kentucky offers a pour of Old Forester and Abita Amber). If you like your whiskey straight, you can choose from several flights created by the bar. Kenton's is pretty upscale, but the $11 price tag for the flights makes it easy to do a comparison and find a favorite. Or, feel free to create your own flight from the more than 150 whiskeys they offer.

Kenton's is a popular spot, and the bar can easily fill up with people waiting for a table, but if you are already Uptown and you have a hankering to try some really special whiskeys, it's worth nudging your way to the bar. I've been on nights when the bar was jam packed, but I've also stopped in closer to happy hour or after the dinner rush and easily found a spot at the bar. According to our bartender, she has already acquired a set of regulars who often stop in after having dinner in the area to have a whiskey nightcap. If you want to end classy, come here.

THE KINGPIN
1307 Lyons St. • (504) 891-2373
www.facebook.com/The-Kingpin
HOURS 3:30 p.m.–til 7 days a week
HAPPY HOUR 3:30–9 p.m. 7 days a week

I really love the Kingpin. It's the kind of place where the bartender calls you "hon." The vibe is punk rockabilly, though the crowd may not have as much ink as that sensibility would indicate. Just as medieval churches were covered with sacred relics and decor to lure pilgrims, the Kingpin is similarly crammed with secular relics: hubcaps, record jackets from Bob Wills and Frank Sinatra, sundry images of Elvis. Installed behind the bar are two velvet paintings: one of Jesus Christ, the other of Hulk Hogan. They're given equal prominence and are each illuminated by the multiple strands of Christmas lights the bar uses in lieu of candles. The red walls lend it a decadent air. The patrons of the Kingpin tend to skew a bit older: few college students, more thirty- and forty-somethings who live nearby. Beer is the focus here, though the wine selection isn't bad. The beer goes well with the myriad food trucks that are usually parked outside. When Lee lived Uptown, this was his neighborhood bar, and though we don't come here often, I always have a good time when we do. It's one of the few bars with shuffleboard, so we usually play a round. Darts are also an option if you need something to do, but ladies beware: one of the boards is hung very near the entrance to your restroom. Just be mindful of errant throws when coming and going!

LE BON TEMPS

4801 Magazine St. • (504) 895-8117
www.facebook.com/le.b.roule
HOURS 3 p.m.–til 7 days a week

Le Bon Temps is really two bars, kind of sewn together. The main bar is a one-room affair, dominated by two pool tables that occupy most of the floor. The room is ringed by rough-hewn wooden booths and long tables from which patrons can watch the games in play. All of the tables have been "inked up" by patrons, with inscriptions pronouncing affection for their beloved, hate for their enemies, or reminders that "New Orleans is Awesome!" It's like bathroom graffiti, but for all to see. Look up and you'll see a giant alligator crawling out of the ceiling. A good test of how drunk you are is how animated the gator seems. If he looks like he is about to eat you, then you should probably switch to beer. Gathered around the bar is a local crowd that the bartender knows well. It's the kind of place where the sandwich board sign outside the door asserts, "You can't drink all day if you don't start in the morning." All in all, the front room of Le Bon Temps a pretty typical New Orleans neighborhood bar.

Then there's the back. On Thursday nights, the back room brims with college students who have gathered to watch brass bands. The back room is smaller than the front room, and when those two groups of people are crammed into that tiny space, the cacophony is intense. I tend to avoid Le Bon Temps on Thursdays, though I understand its appeal, especially to visitors. The rest of the weekend usually features live acts as well. Le Bon Temps also serves up crawfish when in season and free oysters on Friday nights. From a health standpoint, I prefer to pay for my oysters, but free bivalves are a sweet deal if you want to roll the dice. For me, I stick with the Bon Temps on a Monday or Tuesday, when the pool tables are free, the bar is just a little full, and the vibe is chill, all under the benevolent gaze of the alligator.

MAYFAIR LOUNGE

1505 Amelia St. • (504) 895-9163

www.facebook.com/The-Mayfair-Lounge

HOURS noon–2 a.m. 7 days a week

HAPPY HOUR noon–8 p.m. 7 days a week

A friend once referred to the Mayfair as "Snake and Jake's with a mort-gage," but I think that does the bar a bit of a disservice. Though the May-fair's late hours can draw a similar late-late-night (read: early morning) crowd, the vibe of the Mayfair is a little more cheerful. The multitudinous Christmas and Mardi Gras decorations (kept up year-round) lend it a cel-ebratory air.

This little slice of a bar manages to cram in a lot of people, all of whom seem to be laughing and dancing under a canopy of tinsel and spangles. But the true heartbeat of the bar is that of the bon vivant owner, Mrs. Gertrude Mayfield. She and her husband took over the lease of the bar back in 1978. She had been drinking at the bar with him since the early 1960s, a time when women weren't really welcome in bars. They only had the bar for five years when he passed away, and since then the Mayfair has been Mrs. Ger-tie's. She is the doyenne of the place, slinging drinks and keeping folks in line while making sure they all have a great time. As she noted in an interview for the Southern Foodways Alliance, "I'm not here to serve people to get drunk. I'm here to have a nice place—safe place—for people to come and enjoy themselves."

I hate to break it to Mrs. Gertie, but many, many people are getting drunk in your bar. It's easy to do when the drinks are cheap and strong. The Mayfair is where you go when the Delachaise or Columns have closed up for the night and you want to keep going. It's where you keep drinking when you probably should go home. No matter. Though the crowd can get a little bro-heavy, the bros are generally good company. There's something conviv-ial about drinking in the small, cramped space with holiday decor swaying precariously overhead. Like prom, but everyone is drinking legally. You have to press the door buzzer to get in, a security measure from old times. But as my friend Anthony wryly observed, "Every time the doorbell buzzes, an angel gets its wings."

ST. JOE'S

5535 Magazine St. • (504) 899-3744

www.stjoesbar.com

HOURS 5 p.m.–1 a.m. Mon–Wed; 5 p.m.–2 a.m. Thu; 5 p.m.–3 a.m. Fri;
noon–3 a.m. Sat; 6 p.m.–1 a.m. Sun

HAPPY HOUR 5 p.m.–8 p.m. 7 days a week

St. Joseph, the father of Jesus, is one of New Orleans's favorite saints. The patron saint of carpenters, his patronage is sought when one is buying, selling or repairing a house. After Katrina, signs asking for his prayers and intercession peppered the flooded landscape. His feast day, March 19, is marked by many St. Joseph altars, which are laden with food and dismantled to feed the poor. So it was inevitable that eventually there would be a bar opened in his honor. Entering the bar feels like going to church if churches made delicious mojitos. (N.B. I'd be a much better Baptist if they did.) Gilt mirrors adorn the walls and church pew benches offer patrons seating. A portrait of St. Joseph dominates the long narrow bar. According to the bartender, the owners acquired the painting for a song and planned on hanging it in their yet unnamed bar. After spending more than they bargained to restore it, they figured "What the hell?" and named the bar in the saint's honor.

Order their signature mojito (blueberry or original, your choice) and settle in for a visit or a game of pool. If you head to the back patio, the decor changes. The back bar (not always open) is dominated by massive armoire in an indeterminate Asian style. Maybe it's Thai. Maybe it's Indonesian. It does not look like it's from a place where they serve mojitos. No matter; it's still pretty. Colored lanterns hang from the ceiling, and the whole patio has a soft glow. Amid this scene of tranquil beauty, Lee points to some bushes in the corner and reports that he once got really sick there after his fifth mojito. A cautionary tale. He advises no more than three. I agree.

CHAPTER 8

Central City

entral City is a sweeping geographic area that actually comprises several neighborhoods. It was the home of Buddy Bolden, whose face adorns banners hanging on light posts throughout the area. Known as King Bolden, he was a key figure in the development of jazz in New Orleans. Central City was once a thriving area with a bustling economy, and the city market that served it was a community hub. Over time, Central City's fortunes declined, and the neighborhood slid into blight and disrepair. But recent efforts have injected new life into Central City. Oretha Castle Haley is a major artery running through the neighborhood, and businesses have been springing up along that corridor. One, the Southern Food and Beverage Museum, has opened in the former city market, and that once abandoned building is bustling again. Moving along toward Uptown, you can find similar growth along Freret Street. Central City and Freret are both finding their way back to becoming places of prosperity, and bars in both neighborhoods are doing their part to help them along.

BRUNING'S BAR AT THE SOUTHERN FOOD AND BEVERAGE MUSEUM

1504 Oretha Castle Haley Blvd. • (504) 324-6020
www.southernfood.org
HOURS 11 a.m.–5:30 p.m. Wed–Mon
NO HAPPY HOUR

Bruning's was a famous/venerable New Orleans establishment/institution that opened in 1859 and sat on Lake Pontchartrain. Teodor Bruning had purchased a beautiful wooden bar that was built almost a decade before. When the Katrina hit in 2005, the restaurant and its bar sank into the lake.

Though the restaurant was gone, the bar was salvaged by the Bruning family, who donated it to the Southern Food and Beverage Museum. In 2009, the museum restored the bar, and today visitors to the museum can have a drink at this beauty, which is constructed of numerous types of wood and has faux-marble colonettes.

The museum itself is also home to the Museum of the American Cocktail, an extensive collection of cocktail paraphernalia and collectables which recount the evolution of the cocktail in the United States. What could be more New Orleans than walking around a museum about cocktails while sipping on one of your very own? At press time, the museum was about to welcome a new restaurant tenant, and the name had not been announced, so when you go, the name of the venue may be different, but the experience will be just as delightful.

CURE

4905 Freret St. • (504) 302-2357
www.curenola.com
HOURS 5 p.m.–midnight Sun–Thu; 5 p.m.–2 a.m. Fri and Sat
HAPPY HOUR 5 p.m.–7 p.m. Mon–Thu; 3 p.m.–7 p.m. Fri–Sun

Before Hurricane Katrina, there were three kinds of bars in New Orleans: Bourbon Street for getting crazy, neighborhood bars for everyday drinking, and classic spots if you were feeling upscale. Of course, there were bars that pushed these boundaries, but many spots fell within these three. The city was accustomed to these options and, as in many aspects of its culture, was suspicious of anything outside them. After Katrina, the paradigm shifted. With 80 percent of the city under water, it become possible to imagine new directions for pretty much every aspect of life. While many folks were rethinking what schools should look like, what City Hall should become, or hell, what the city itself should become, some folks were rethinking what drinking here could be.

Cure opened in 2008 and was one the first of this new kind of bar that offered the city a new way of drinking. The first time I visited, everything about that bar felt unfamiliar, and I wasn't sure if I liked it. The drinks had names I had never heard of. They had ingredients I had never heard of. They certainly took longer to make than any drink I had ever ordered. And the care and attention the bartenders took in making the drinks felt unfamiliar. There was a dress code (no shorts), and people were actually asked to leave if they weren't dressed up to snuff. I thought that was rude. Some of their servers were not friendly when you asked them to explain any portion of the menu. Much as I struggle with the southern obsession with hospitality, I found this exclusionary stance distasteful. Even the design of the bar felt, well, foreign. Its subway tile felt straight from New York, and its Edison lights were not yet common. Even its name, Cure, which pointed to cocktails' historic connection with pharmacies, was odd.

But then I had a drink. It was amazing. This was certainly not the Old Fashioned that I had been sipping on ever since my mother let me try hers when I was still a child. And I understood then what this new category of bar was: cocktail bar. And for good or bad, I knew that drinking in the

So many spirits at Cure

city was going to change. But since then, Cure has changed a bit, too. They ditched the dress code. Owner Neal Bodenheimer acknowledges its enforcement might not have won them friends, but at the time they were trying to set themselves apart as a new game in town. They have also worked on training the staff to be more approachable, and though you can still get that guy who only makes a face if you order Crown Royal (which they don't have), you are more likely to get someone who gently recommends another whiskey. The only common link between my observations about Cure back then and Cure now is that they still serve amazing drinks. In the eight years I have been drinking there, I've never had a bad drink.

Cure brought New Orleans another kind of drinking that is now so much a part of the city's scene, many of us have forgotten what a big deal it was when they opened up.

THE OTHER BAR

5039 Freret St. • (504) 231-7011
www.facebook.com/otherbaronfreret
HOURS 4 p.m.–midnight Sun–Thu; 4 p.m.–2 a.m. Fri and Sat
HAPPY HOUR 4 p.m.–8 p.m. 7 days a week

This quirky joint is a great spot to pop in after filling up at Dat Dog across the street. Reclaimed wood in multitudinous colors makes up a charming bar, tables, and even part of the ceiling. Board games strewn across picnic tables invite patrons to linger. You can also try your luck at the vintage Ms. Pacman or skee-ball court. A friend observed that one table in particular would be perfect for D&D. The garage sale decor might seem like it's trying too hard in other incarnations, but here, it really does feel like somebody cleaned out their mom's hall closet and decided to open a bar for their friends. The beer selection includes some local and regional brews. The cocktail list is small and quirky, just like its setting, and I'm a sucker for any list that offers a Singapore Sling. You can also sample one of their rotating draft cocktails; the whiskey/ginger was a favorite. The Other Bar also lets you bring in food, so you often see folks snacking on hot dogs from Dat Dog across the street or a sandwich from Liberty Cheesesteaks down the block.

For all of you who like to "go green," the Other Bar is one of the few spots in New Orleans that has upped its sustainability game. They serve canned

Reclaimed wooden bar at the quirky Other Bar

Neal Bodenheimer

When Neal Bodenheimer decided to leave New York and open a bar in his hometown of New Orleans in 2008, he never imagined that a place he envisioned as a neighborhood bar would grow to become one of the most respected bars in the world. He never even thought Cure would be a destination, much less receive a James Beard nomination for Outstanding Bar Program, several Tales of the Cocktail Spirited Award nominations, or be named one of the world's fifty best bars by Drinks International. When Cure opened, these ideas never existed in the industry, and as Bodenheimer notes, "The industry changed as we were starting, and we were in the right place at the right time."

The right place turned out to be Freret Street, which in 2008 was a barren corridor. I asked him how he feels when people say that Cure was an anchor for Freret's revival, and he acknowledged that Cure was the one of the first businesses to make a significant financial investment in that area. "We were ahead of arts and culture overlay," he concedes, "but it would have eventually happened." Bodenheimer had initially planned to open his bar in New York, but after Katrina, felt a strong pull to come back and aid his city in its recovery. And though he changed his location, he never changed his vision. Cure was going to be a New York cocktail bar, and the drinks were going to be great, no excuses. Bodenheimer considers himself to be a champion of New Orleans culture, but unlike some locals, he doesn't put it on a pedestal.

I agree with Bodenheimer's assessment of the cocktail scene before Katrina. "New Orleans seemed torn between progress and preservation, and pre-Katrina, was maybe too far towards preservation. Minus a few stalwarts," he recalls, "it was hard to get a decent cocktail in town." He remembers that it was even hard to get a decent Sazerac, the city's official cocktail. But he also points out the drink itself never disappeared. He notes, "It was still made here, because we are preservationist at heart, but it didn't mean we did it well." Now there are dozens of cocktail bars making not only delicious Sazeracs, but other well-crafted drinks as well. And Cure played a role in shifting that paradigm.

beer over glass bottles so they can then recycle the cans, and they also use compostable to-go cups and bamboo stirrers. Even their use of reclaimed wood puts them in the "renew, reuse, recycle" camp. What could make your drink taste better than knowing you are helping to save the planet?

VERRET'S

1738 Washington Ave. • (504) 895-9640
www.verretslounge.com
HOURS 4 p.m.–til 7 days a week
NO HAPPY HOUR

As my friend visiting from Los Angeles observed, "This is a great bar that hasn't been ruined yet." Verret's is a neighborhood bar under new management, and though they gave the bar a total makeover, the atmosphere and crowd it draws feel like they've been exactly like this for years. The red naugahyde bar is a delight: classic old-school. Banners for various Mardi Gras Indian tribes and social aid and pleasure clubs hang on the walls, including that of the Fabulous Ladies Social Aid and Pleasure club. The prices fit Verret's moniker as a neighborhood joint: $3 for a beer and craft cocktails like the Bulleit Old Fashioned for $7. The crowd is all local, and most are familiar to the bartender. One patron, still in his security guard uniform, nurses a beer at the edge of the bar while charging his phone into a power strip that the bartender has pulled out specifically for his use. We sip our first drinks under the red light of the fringed lanterns hanging above the bar, envying those who are nestled in the cushy red booths, then take round two outside to the patio.

Service industry folks smoke under a school of sea creature light fixtures made from melted Mardi Gras beads. We find a picnic bench under a green and orange octopus, swimming through the air toward a jellyfish. Wednesdays and Thursdays, the bar thumps to the sounds of bands like Chapter Soul, but on a Monday, Verrett's is a good place to visit with friends. We imagine it's more fun to bartend when the crowd is dancing on the black and white checkerboard floor and the bar is booming with music. When we asked our bartender, Ed, if he wished it were busier, he demurred. He prefers nights like this when he can easily chat with new patrons and regulars. "I like it when we're not making too much money."

CHAPTER 9

Riverbend and Carrollton

T his part of the city was originally owned by Chauvin de la Frenière. Back in 1769, he participated in a revolt against the Spanish government, which controlled Louisiana at the time. Spain had forbidden the importation of French goods and required locals to only buy Spanish goods. Among the French products no longer available were French cognac and French wine. As you can imagine, this was not a popular law. He led a group of four hundred locals (most of whom had been drinking) into what is now Jackson Square. Allegedly, they yelled, "Give us back our Bordeaux; take away the poison of Catalonia." La Frenière and the other leaders of this revolt were rounded up and hanged.

After his death, the land was eventually incorporated into a town, named in honor of General Carroll, a leader in the Battle of New Orleans. New Orleans annexed the town in 1875, but the residents retained a strong sense of their previous status as an independent locale. The "Mayor of Carrollton" remained an informal title until 1984 and was held by a resident who spoke on behalf of the neighborhood's needs to the New Orleans City Council. Carrollton is near enough to Loyola and Tulane Universities to cater to that crowd, but if you are willing to overlook some of the more college-focused watering holes, it offers its own kind of neighborhood charm.

ALE
8124 Oak St. • (504) 324-6558
www.facebook.com/aleonoak

The taps of Ale

HOURS 5 p.m.–11 p.m. Mon and Tue; 5 p.m.–midnight Wed; 5 p.m.–1 a.m. Thur;
2 p.m.–2 a.m. Fri; 1 p.m.–2 a.m. Sat; 1 p.m.–11 p.m. Sun
HAPPY HOUR 5 p.m.–7 p.m. Mon–Thur

Ale is one of several new beer bars that have opened in New Orleans in the last few years. Its thirty taps rotate regularly, with an array of local, regional, and national craft beers guaranteed to please everyone's palate. Ale isn't a sports bar, but it's certainly sports-friendly. The owners have managed to shoehorn in six TVs, tonight tuned to anything from the NHL Finals to the Copa America tournament. Billed as "upscale dive," it is neither. It's too casual to be upscale and too clean and new to be a dive, though the worn wooden floors, salvaged from the now defunct Dixie Brewery, give it the kind of patina a beer bar needs. The paintings of monkeys drinking beer hanging in the bathroom hallway add a quirky touch and made me think of those paintings of dogs playing poker that neighborhood bars like to display.

While Ale may not have a large beer list, it is thoughtfully curated. The bartender told us that the owner is committed to serving "interesting beers," and the bar has featured hard-to-get pours of local beers like Parish's Ghost in the Machine and several sours from Great Raft. Each night features a special, with Monday Flight Nights a personal favorite. If you are in the mood for something with a higher proof, their American whiskey and Scotch whisky lists are remarkably strong, given the rather small size of the bar. The kitchen turns out solid gastropub fare and stays open late. Ale gets a lot of tourists who are waiting for a table at Jaques Imo's (a popular restaurant down the street) or waiting for a show at the Maple Leaf club, but the majority of their patrons are locals who live nearby. If you get tired of beer or whiskey, step out onto their side patio and walk over to Oak, the wine bar next door, the sister bar of Ale. Beer, whiskey, wine. They've got all the bases covered.

COOTER BROWN'S

509 S. Carrollton Ave. • (504) 866-9104
HOURS 11 a.m.–1 a.m. or 2 a.m.
HAPPY HOUR 3 p.m.–7 p.m.

I've been drinking at Cooter Brown's since 1995, but it took writing a book about the bars of the city to prompt me to wonder, "Who the hell is Cooter Brown?" Depending on your point of view, Cooter Brown was a wastrel or a genius. He lived on the boundary of the Union and Confederacy during the Civil War. This position made him eligible for draft by both camps. According to legend, he either had family on each side (or didn't want to pick in case he chose the wrong position), so he decided to get drunk and stay drunk in order to be declared "unfit for military service." The plan worked, and "drunk as Cooter Brown" has remained a benchmark for intoxication since.

If you are a beer fan, it is not hard not to follow the fellow's lead at his

Just three of the many clever celebrity and beer sculptures at Cooter Brown's

namesake bar. Cooter Brown's has more than forty rotating taps and four hundred bottles, serving regional, national and international brews. It was one of the first bars in New Orleans to make its beer list a feature, and it has remained in the vanguard of beer bars since.

Cooter Brown's also features some of my favorite bar decor in the city: The Celebrity Hall of Foam and Beersoleum. Lined up along the tops of the walls are one hundred caricature statues of dead celebrities (about eighteen inches tall), each clutching a beer bottle that bears some relationship to his or her fame. Richard Nixon brandishes a Tsing Tao, Louis Armstrong offers a bottle of Dixie, Bob Marley grips a Red Stripe, and Alfred Hitchcock presents a Dead Guy. All were crafted by artist Scott Conary, who once worked in the Cooter Brown's kitchen.

Cooter Brown's is also a sports bar; twenty televisions line the walls. On game days, pockets of fans crowd around the TV showing their team. The steady cacophony of the matches is punctuated from all corners by whoops of delight or groans of despair as different teams score or falter throughout the day.

Cooter Brown's recently changed hands and is now under the direction of the same folks who operate the Rusty Nail. In a recent interview, they promised to keep Cooter Brown's exactly as it is, a friendly, neighborhood sports bar with one of the best beer lists in town. They did admit, though, that they might dust the statues once in awhile.

OAK

8118 Oak St. • (504) 302-1485
www.oaknola.com
HOURS 5 p.m.–til Tue–Sat
HAPPY HOUR 5 p.m.–7 p.m. Tue–Sat

Most wine bars tend to evoke an Italian enoteca style. With its cool white walls and contemporary lighting, Oak Wine Bar looks like an art gallery that decided to toss out the "no red wine" policy and plop a bar in its center. Oak shares a patio with its sister bar, Ale, but the venues could not be more different. While Ale is narrow and small, Oak is cavernous and can easily host several sets of birthday celebrants in the curtained niches that line its sides. While the ratio of TVs to empty wall space in Ale seems about 1:1, Oak has only two TVs, and even those get lost among numerous modern art paintings. The atmosphere is lively, even noisy, as voices bounce around the vaulted ceiling. Everyone is having a good time; the wine, of course, is helping.

Oak offers its patrons a selection of hundreds of wines by the glass, and unlike most wine menus that are organized by region, Oak's menu is grouped by palate notes like "Stones and Roses," "Herbs and Smoke," and "Bolder Chords." My favorite nights are Wednesdays: half-price bottles! If you come with a group, arrive early enough to commandeer one corner of the room and spread out on the cushy banquettes. On weekends, even a spacious bar like Oak can fill, especially when the band gets started. If you need a breather, step out onto the patio and enjoy a well-priced glass of bubbly.

SNAKE AND JAKE'S CHRISTMAS CLUB LOUNGE

7612 Oak St. • (504) 861-2802
HOURS 7 p.m.–til 7 days a week
HAPPY HOUR 7 p.m.–10 p.m. 7 days a week

It seems a kind of boozy miracle that Snake and Jake's is still around. The kinds of bars that people open today (and presumably the kinds of bars where people want to drink) are the opposite of Snake & Jake's. They are curated. They have cocktail menus. Their decor is planned and intentional. They are "charming" or "elegant" or "hip." Drinking at Snake and Jake's feels like drinking in a trailer whose walls are painted black and whose sole illumination comes from a few strings of Christmas lights. There is a very tired looking sofa with a dog sleeping on it. The space is dark, but not in a "cool" way. It is dark because that's the best environment for the kind of drinking you are going to do here: cheap, determined, early morning drinking. There are no windows, and Snake and Jake's is not unlike a casino—you quickly lose all sense of time. You could easily emerge from this cavern sometime in the next year, like a latter-day Rip Van Winkle. This is another one of those bars where I didn't plan to drink, but I did anyway (see Pal's in Mid-City). My past visits to Snake and Jake's were, frankly, a blur, and they usually happened around at 3 a.m. when it was crowded with students or the recently graduated. But for this visit, we arrived before midnight, and discovered the earlier crowd (11 p.m.) is a slightly older crowd. Also, the bar was pretty empty, which gave me time to chat with Jay, who has tended bar here for six years. How do you get to be a bartender at Snake and Jake's? It helps if you live nearby and drink here a lot. Eventually they ask if you want to pick up some shifts. I also learned the origin of the rather odd name.

There were once two bars located very near to each other: Snake's Christmas Club (Snake was his nickname, Christmas was his last name) and Jake's Lounge. They combined into this venue, which was originally Snake's Club. I could have stayed at Snake and Jake's for several more rounds. I probably felt like I could do this because I had never arrived at Snake and Jake's this early or this sober (two drinks in). But instead I called it after one whiskey and soda. On my way out, the bouncer addressed the dog, who was following him around, saying, "You know you are supposed to be on the sofa." And the rest of us, presumably, should be at the bar.

BARS OF NEW ORLEANS BY CATEGORY

ROMANTIC BARS
1. Bombay Club
2. French 75
3. Loa
4. Sylvain
5. The Columns

HISTORIC BARS
1. Carousel Bar
2. Sazerac Bar
3. Lafitte's Blacksmith Shop
4. The Columns
5. The Napoleon House
6. Tujague's

BARS WITH BEAUTIFUL COURTYARDS
1. Bacchanal
2. Brennan's
3. Cane & Table
4. Empire Bar at Broussard's
5. Oxalis
6. Pat O'Brien's

LATE-NIGHT BARS FOR WELL-MADE COCKTAILS
1. Bar Tonique
2. Bourbon O
3. Cure

4. Oxalis' The Branch (on weekends)
5. The Black Penny
6. Twelve Mile Limit

BARS WITH A ROOFTOP VIEW
1. Alto at the ACE Hotel
2. Hot Tin bar at the Pontchartrain Hotel
3. Catahoula Rooftop

CHEAP DIVE BARS WHERE YOU CAN FORGET YOUR NAME
1. Kajun's
2. Club Ms. Mae's
3. Snake and Jake's Christmas Club Lounge
4. Saturn Bar
5. The Abbey
6. The Mayfair
7. The Saint

BARS WITH GREAT WHISKEY LISTS
1. Avenue Pub
2. Barrel Proof
3. Bourbon House
4. D.B.A.
5. Kenton's

BARS WITH GREAT RUM LISTS
1. Black Duck
2. Cane & Table
3. El Libre
4. Latitude 29
5. Tiki Tolteca

BARS WITH GREAT BEER LISTS
1. Ale
2. Avenue Pub

3. Aline Street Beer Garden
4. Bayou Beer Garden
5. Cooter Brown's
6. Junction
7. The Bulldog

BARS WITH GREAT WINE
1. Bayou Wine Garden
2. Delachaise
3. Mimi's in the Marigny
4. N7
5. Oak
6. Tasting Room
7. W.I.N.O.

BARS WITH AMAZING COCKTAILS
1. Bar Tonique
2. Bouligny Tavern
3. Compere Lapin
4. Cure
5. Empire Bar
6. French 75
7. Revel

APPENDIX II
BREWERIES

Louisiana is a bit late to the craft-brewing scene, but is doing its best to catch up. Several new breweries have opened up recently and most are open to the public for some on-the-spot imbibing. The level of finish on their bars varies widely; most merely have a small bar attached to their brewing warehouse.

Garden District

COURTYARD BREWERY
1020 Erato St. • No phone
www.courtyardbrewing.com
HOURS 4 p.m.–10 p.m. Mon–Wed; 11 a.m.–10 p.m. Thu–Sun
NO HAPPY HOUR

Courtyard's taproom is set in the warehouse parking lot, but it's a charming parking lot, with Christmas lights strung about and spools once used to hold industrial cables serving as tables. Courtyard pours its own brews as well as other craft beers from around the country. Food trucks park here every night but Mondays, when you can bring your own food.

URBAN SOUTH BREWERY
1645 Tchoupitoulas St. • (504) 517-4677
urbansouthbrewery.com
HOURS 4 p.m.–8 p.m. Thu–Fri; noon–8 p.m. Sat–Sun
NO HAPPY HOUR

This bar is inside their warehouse, which means it's mighty hot in the summer, but once the weather cools, it's a fun place to stop in and sample their specialty beers and any food trucks that may be parked there. You can try their flagship beers and specialty projects, all poured in their signature mason jar glasses. Urban South offers brewery tours every day they are open; check their website for times. Their space is also kid and dog friendly.

Uptown

NOLA BREWERY AND TAP ROOM
3001 Tchoupitoulas St. • (504) 301-0117
www.nolabrewing.com/tap-room
HOURS 11 a.m.–11 p.m. Mon–Sun
NO HAPPY HOUR

Nola Brewery offers the most built-out taproom of all the local breweries. The Tap Room would be a great place to come with a group, especially if you are here with a bachelor party. The back of the bar houses ping-pong and foosball tables, as well as a cornhole court. The upstairs bar also leads to the balcony, with a great view of the river and the trains rolling by. Though you can find Nola beers throughout the city, if you want to try their specialty offerings, you will need to do so here. McClure's BBQ makes a good base for the beer. You can come here after a Friday brewery tour and stay till long after the sun sets.

Mid-City

SECOND LINE BREWING
433 N. Bernadotte St. • (504) 248-8979
www.secondlinebrewing.com
HOURS Wed–Fri 4 p.m.–10 p.m.; Sat noon–10 p.m.; Sun noon–8 p.m.

This brewery is set along the Lafitte Greenway, a public park–like path that connects Tremé with Mid-City. The brewery has decked out its parking lot like a beer garden with ample tables for groups to gather. Visitors can leave with growlers filled with their flagship brews or sip on specialty pints. Periodic movie nights feature films projected on the wall of the warehouse. Food trucks are there each day they are open, with the menu listed online.

504 CRAFT BEER

3939 Tulane Ave. • (504) 875-3723
504craftbeer.com
HOURS 11 a.m.–7 p.m. 7 days a week

This bottle shop has the largest selection of craft beers in the city and also keeps 6 taps in heavy rotation for you to fill up your growlers. They allow customers to sample their tapped beers at tastings hosted in the store several days a week, and they will be expanding these sampling times as well. Though not a brewery, they could be your one stop for bringing home beer from all of Louisiana's regional breweries.

APPENDIX III
WINE STORES WITH BARS

Each of the following locations is primarily a wine shop, but also has a bar where patrons can purchase wines by the glass. All allow patrons to purchase bottles to drink on the premises for a small fee.

Marigny

FAUBOURG WINE

2805 Saint Claude Ave. • (504) 342-2217
www.fauborgwines.com
HOURS 12 p.m.–9 p.m. Sun–Thu; 12 p.m.–10 p.m. Fri–Sat

Located near the train tracks that divide the Marigny from the Bywater, this charming spot usually offers a selection of four to five wines by the glass, one of which is almost always sparkling. They offer a small selection of cheese and bread if you need a nibble, and their beer selection is solid, in case your friends prefer brew to vino. Free wine tastings every Wednesdays.

Mid-City

SWIRL WINE BAR & MARKET

3143 Ponce de Leon Street • (504) 304-0635
www.swirlnola.com/
HOURS 12 p.m.–8 p.m. Mon; 11 a.m.–8 p.m. Tue–Thu; 11 a.m.–9 p.m. Fri; 11 a.m.–9 p.m. Sat

This tiny shop just off Esplanade Avenue pours more than twenty wines by the glass, which means they have something for everyone. Hungry patrons can nosh on small Mediterranean-inspired plates supplied by Swirl's next-door neighbor, 100 Figs. Check out their event listings for classes and tastings.

PEARL WINE CO.

3700 Orleans Ave. Ste. 1C • (504) 483-6314
www.pearlwineco.com
HOURS Noon–8 p.m. Sun; Noon–midnight Mon–Sat
HAPPY HOUR Check website for different drink specials Mon–Fri

Pearl Wine Co bills itself as four thousand square feet of beverage paradise. Located on Bayou St. John in the American Can Company (once a warehouse and now an apartment building), the store not only pours more than twenty-five wines by the glass, but also has a full bar. Their craft beer selection is equally robust.

CREDITS

p. 6, 16, 23, 43, 167, 170 – Photography by Kevin O'Mara

p. 8 – © Peter Vilsimaa / iStockphoto.com

p. 24 – © f11photo / Shutterstock

p. 30 – © Arnaud's Restaurant / Brian F. Huff 2011

p. 32 – Photography by Mark Schettler

p. 33 – Photography by Will Crocker; © Beachbum Berry's Latitude 29

p. 36, 50, – Courtesy of Creole Restaurant Concepts

p. 38, 40 – Photography by Sara Schulenberg; Courtesy of Dickie Brennan & Co.

p. 45 – Photography provided by Hotel Manteleone

p. 49 – Photography by Bazil Zerinsky

p. 52, 103 – Photography by Lee Domingue

p. 54, 135 – Courtesy of Galatoire's

p. 57 – Photography by Wendy Chatalain

p. 62 – Photography by Calli Folse

p. 65 – Photography by Michael Palumbo

p. 68, 137 – Courtesy of the Commander's Palace Family of Restaurants

p. 69, 142, 154, 160 – Photography by Rush Jagoe

p. 71 – Photography by Sam Hanna/Hannaphoto; Courtesy of Mark Latter, owner

p. 73 – Photography by Jennifer Mitchell; Courtesy of Ann Tunnerman

p. 78 – © Rick Lord Photography / iStockphoto.com

p. 84, 86, 99 – Photography by Cheryl Gerber

p. 95 – Photography by Angela Eve & Anastasios Ketsios Image Collective

p. 100 – © lightphoto / iStockphoto.com

p. 104 – Photography by Robert Clark

p. 108 – Photography by Jeanne Palazzo; David Demarest, owner

p. 110, 115, 118 – Photography by Tyler Chauvin

p. 112 – Ralph Brennan Restaurant Group

p. 120 – © Sean Pavone / Shutterstock

p. 127 – Photography by Madeleine Rose; Courtesy of Windsor Court

p. 129 – Photography by Star Chefs; Courtesy of Teresa Shaun, Brustman Carrino PR on behalf of Compere Lapin

ALPHABETICAL INDEX

view, bars with rooftop, 180
Volstead Act, 19
Voodoo, The, 75

W

W (hotel), bar, 67–68
Walter, Alan, 131, 133
Warehouse District, 121–38
   about, 121
   bars, 121–38
Watts, Polly, 140–41, 146
Wecklein, Chris, 92
Wednesdays at the Square, 123

Westmorland, Kurt, 128
whiskey lists, bars with great, 180
Williams, Tennessee, 79, 144–45
Windsor Court Cocktail Bar,
      126–28
wine, bars with great, 181
wine stores with bars, 187–88
W.I.N.O. (Wine Institute of New
      Orleans), 137–38

Y

Yseult, Sean, 148
Yuki Izakaya, 98

NEIGHBORHOOD INDEX

WAREHOUSE DISTRICT.